Farther West

New World

Farther West
New World

John Murrell

Coach House Press, Toronto

Published with the assistance of the Canada Council
and the Ontario Arts Council.

ISBN 0-88910-289-9

Photo Credits

p. 16 George Gammon
p. 32 Keith James
p. 36 George Gammon
p. 54 George Gammon
All photographs of *New World* are by Robert C. Rasdale,
FRPS. The photograph of John Murrell is by Lincoln
Steffens.

CONTENTS

AN INTRODUCTION

by Urjo Kareda

These two extraordinary plays by John Murrell take very different journeys but they arrive at the same place – literally, the shores of the Pacific Ocean: English Bay in *Farther West* and China Beach in *New World*. They are both edge-of-the-continent plays, and their shared impulse is toward some world beyond the frontier. This sense of personality and destiny lived out on the *edge* provides the plays with their intensity and urgency. John Murrell's characters don't give themselves too many chances; they insist upon acting out the full implications of the instant.

These plays which end at the same place have very different origins. *Farther West* (first produced in 1982 and substantially revised in 1985: it is the new version which is printed here) began with a newspaper clipping describing an actual *crime passionel* in which a Calgary prostitute, May Buchanan, and her lover barricaded themselves in a hotel-room and murdered one another. This was the fact from which *Farther West* grew, and grew away, but the real beginnings of the play, in my opinion, go back to the late 1970s, when John Murrell was commissioned by the Stratford Festival to write a play called *Parma*. This work was to be a wholly free and independent adaptation of the plot of John Ford's *'Tis Pity She's a Whore*, and as John Murrell and I discussed the work at length over several months, it was clear that he was eager to explore in epic terms the widest possible range of sensual experience and erotic obsession, and how these crack apart a social order. As it turned out, *Parma* remained unfinished Stratford Festival business, but the playwright's fixation with the themes of sex and freedom was clearly transported into another epic play, which became *Farther West*. The Canadian West in the last decades of the nineteenth century is worlds away from an Italian Renaissance court, just as the erotic identity of a woman in her

7

prime is worlds away from the sexuality of adolescent siblings, but the white heat of desire that Murrell wanted to capture survived the transition between these worlds. And survived *blazing*.

Farther West spans six years, 1886 to 1892, and travels from Rat Portage (now Kenora), Ontario, via the Northwest Territories, to British Columbia. On the other hand, *New World* (first produced in 1985) covers only twelve hours and never moves out of sight of China Beach. It is also the first of John Murrell's mature works to be set in the present. The play unfolds and flowers as an elegant, witty comedy, energized by its anger and burnished by its melancholy. The play's siblings – two brothers and a sister, all British-born but having spent their adult lives in different countries – find themselves dragged kicking and screaming into a middle age of warring illusions and delusions. Murrell is a great chronicler, in *New World* as in earlier plays, of the perils of maturity. For just as May Buchanan in *Farther West* eloquently demands the right to a continuing search for discovery, the three Rennies in *New World*, Bob and Bet and Larry, find themselves at the gate of self-discovery and must decide, gingerly and not without panic, whether to pass through. The origins of this work, I believe, come from the playwright's deep affection for and familiarity with the plays of Anton Chekhov. For the Stratford Festival, Murrell wrote new versions of both *Uncle Vanya* and *The Seagull*, which released his affinity for the subtle rhythms, emotional convolutions and beautifully nuanced tone which link *New World* and its Russian predecessors (not forgetting, too, another spinoff, Bernard Shaw's Chekhovian *Heartbreak House*, also an apocalyptic vision filled with brilliant invention and mordant wit).

Two plays, then, which seem so different, and yet two plays which also seem to belong together. In practical terms, of course, both were shaped and realized by the same remarkable director, Robin Phillips. Both plays, too, contain roles specifically written for that most

8

astonishing actor, Martha Henry, whose Cleopatra-like infinite variety would be a miraculous and daunting inspiration for any playwright. (Put the passionate will and fire of May Buchanan beside the nervy drive and wit of Carla Rennie and you will have some small glimmering of this great actor's range of possibilities, and also of this playwright's subtle response to it.)

Both plays are also profoundly informed with John Murrell's passion for music, and, in particular, for opera. To call both plays 'operatic' might be to invite the derision and condescension of those who won't understand and don't love opera. Murrell, however, does know and does understand, and he pours that sensibility into his writing. Both plays contain references to, and fragments from, opera, and both plays have sequences conceived and organized in operatic terms: *Farther West*, for instance, has at least two specifically defined quartets (the laundry scene in Act I, the May-Violet-Hanks-Shepherd scene in Act II), and *New World* contains some splendid trios and duets, as well as a Papageno/Papagena pairing in Peter and Linda. The rapturous final scene in *New World*, filled with music cues, is a culmination of melodic themes, just as *Farther West* has, woven through it, two songs which are modulated like *leitmotifs*. The music in John Murrell's plays – his 'operatic' style, if you will – suggests a more intensified plane of emotion and experience. Opera itself presents a heightening of feeling which, at one and the same time, is taken to the level of the abstract, of pure emotion, and still kept absolutely human because the instrument is the most personal of them all, the voice. So, too, John Murrell's lyric theatre, which is anticipated and supported by the incidence of music itself in his plays, presents both a *stylistic* search for an intensified verbal expression and a *thematic* search for a higher plane of personal existence. His use of music is central and elemental, just like the recurring images of the sea and the sun in both plays (images which also link them to his earlier play *Memoir*). Murrell's texts are filled with naturalistic

9

detail, the sounds of dogs and birds, but as in Chekhov, these sounds are not part of a realistic background but a poetically arranged orchestration complementing the words. Murrell's music offers a similar counterpoint. Indeed, the meaning of *Farther West* cannot really be grasped without a study of its music (both words and music written by the playwright) and how it serves to contrast and support the text, expressing an underlying world of yearning and innocence beneath a violent physical reality.

The plays belong together, too, simply because they seem to be about so many of the same subjects. They show John Murrell's deep-rooted and moving concerns about friendship and family, seen both in the gallant camaraderie of May Buchanan's invented, improvised family, and the shifting, binding disparities within the Rennies' blood ties. They both present societies in which characters who are seen as 'outsiders' – Violet and Carla and even Bet – make their way with courage, crackling wit and bravura. They bring together characters from many different backgrounds – the Canadians, the Americans and those with mysteriously mixed bloods in *Farther West*, the British, the Americans and the Canadians, both English and French, in *New World* – onto the arena of the new west to test themselves against a landscape which offers them everything and nothing. The plays show us worlds exploding; the glass ball in *New World* is an objectification of the way that May Buchanan's world shatters into pieces and cannot be repaired. Both *Farther West* and *New World* celebrate risk and obsession, which is what makes them so complementary, so Canadian, and, as is my belief, so autobiographical. These are plays, above all else, of self-definition. John Murrell thrusts us into the world of those who push themselves to the edges of continents both geographic and emotional, and who, on that brink, discover the wild, and perhaps demented, exhilaration of willingly, wilfully straddling absolute annihilation and total freedom.

Farther West

a romance

CREDITS:

Farther West was first presented by Theatre Calgary (Artistic Director, Rick McNair) on April 22nd, 1982, with the following cast:

MAY BUCHANAN   Martha Henry
A MAN IN BED WITH HER   William Webster
VIOLET DECARMIN   Jackie Burroughs
SEWARD   David Fox
NETTIE MCDOWELL   Sheila McCarthy
TIDWELL*   Stephen Russell
BABCOCK   William Webster
LILY REEVES   Barbara Budd
ROSS   Neil Foster
THOMAS SHEPHERD   Alan Scarfe
RAGLAN   Paul Gross
HANKS   Rod Beattie
VYVYAN*   Keith James
ANNA*   Barbara Budd
OTHERS   Paul Cowling, Roger Duncan, Grant Linneberg, Brent Piaskoski, Steward Stefansson

The play was directed by Robin Phillips, with set and costumes by Daphne Dare, lighting by Allan Stichbury, and musical arrangements by Laura Burton.

* These characters do not appear in the revised version of the script which is published here, as presented by Tarragon Theatre, Toronto, in its 1985-86 season.

CHARACTERS (in order of appearance):

MAY BUCHANAN
A MAN IN BED WITH HER
VIOLET DECARMIN
SEWARD
NETTIE MCDOWELL
BABCOCK
LILY REEVES
ROSS
THOMAS SHEPHERD
RAGLAN
HANKS

The action takes place in Ontario, British Columbia, and in the North West Territories of Canada, between the years 1886 and 1892.

for Martha

Rat Portage, Ontario. Summer, 1886. Afternoon.

A narrow bed. MAY, *in her early thirties, is lying there with a much older man. She is naked. He wears dirty woolen drawers and an undershirt. He is very still, on his stomach, his eyes closed, one arm wrapped around* MAY.

Music: the first act tune, 'Dear Maisie,' played on harmonica, concertina, or piano. (See Music Appendix)

MAY   Next? Next was rich old Mister Leslie, who called me his 'little ray of sunshine.' Because I made his 'posy grow.' [*She laughs.*]

I was fourteen years old. Next? A German boy from Berlin, Ontario. Had shoulders like a gallows-tree, that wide! Held his big hand over my mouth, from start to finish. Afraid I might scream. I wouldn't have. Next? A drill-master from the military academy over in Hull. He whispered his commands into my ear, and I whispered back, 'Yes, sir!' Because that excited him. Next? Well, I took up with a druggist from across the back lane. Because I was scared I'd caught something, and figured he might cure me of it. Turned out I was just getting older, getting to be a woman. He couldn't cure me of that. Next? ... Well, one day my old dad comes into my room. I'm lying there – just exactly as I'm lying here right now – being cuddled by this fellow who sharpens scissors and carts off trash, I think his name was Callaghan. My old dad just stares at me for the longest time. Doesn't gnash his teeth nor tear his hair, like they do in story books. And Christ knows, there's no tears that well up in his aged eyes! Callaghan? He sleeps through the whole thing, of course. And I – I stare right back, straight at my old dad. Don't whimper nor run howling down the hall. Christ knows, I don't fall at his feet to ask forgiveness!

[*As she continues,* MAY *will slowly unwrap the* MAN*'s arm from her waist, get out of bed, and get fully dressed, including stockings, shoes, coat and hat. The* MAN *stirs slightly, but his eyes remain closed.*]

Finally my old dad says: 'You can't carry on like this,

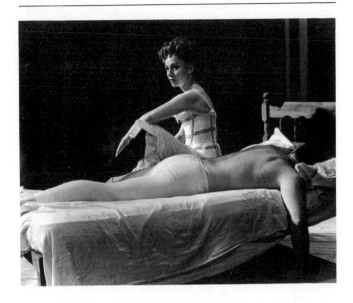

Martha Henry (MAY BUCHANAN) and William Webster (MAN IN BED).

May. Not in my house. Not anymore! You better move on, girl, better start moving, farther west! You travel far enough west,' he says, 'maybe you'll find some Godforsaken place where there's no rules – no laws, no judges. But you mustn't go just to the Red River,' my old dad says. 'You have to go much farther than that! No, not just to the Rocky Mountains or the far Pacific! Not just to China either,' my old dad says. 'China's hardly the start of your journey! Even in China they got such things as manners. Morals! They got certain prescriptions for female behaviour! I tell you what, girl,' he says, 'you'll know you've wandered far enough, when you can knock a man down, right in the street, and climb up on top of him – or he can knock you down, climb on top of you – and the children walk past, and the wagons roll past – and even the stray dogs don't stop nor turn round for a second look at your contaminating presence! Get packed now, May, and move on!' He points out the window, towards the

Methodist Church steeple. 'That way's west,' he says. So
I crawl out from under Callaghan. I get myself dressed, I
get myself packed. I look at my old dad, for the last time.
And I say, 'I can't figure out why everybody around here
thinks you're a halfwit, Dad. I thank you for your wise
and honest advice. At last I got some direction in life!'
And I walk right out. I look around for that steeple. And
I move on! ... Callaghan slept on for hours maybe, there
in my bed. He always slept like the dead afterwards.
Well, most of you are like that!
[*She is nearly dressed by now. She looks down at the* MAN
in the bed.]
So? Is that what you wanted to hear? Ready for the next
exciting chapter? Want to know what happened to me –
right here in Rat Portage – just this morning?
[*She prods him with a finger or a foot. He grunts, smiles.
Maybe he rolls over, but doesn't open his eyes more than
halfway. As* MAY *completes her story, she finishes
dressing, takes a small suitcase from underneath the
bed. She locates a few articles of clothing among the
bedclothes, and throws them into the suitcase. The* MAN*'s
eyes soon close again.*]
Just this morning – right here – down at the dry goods
store, I knew my time had come! I was looking at some
stuff which they call velvet – which isn't velvet at all.
Figuring how many yards of it I could get with two
dollars in silver. All of a sudden, this little mongrel pup
runs right up under my skirts! The little shop clerk's
little mongrel pup! Well, there I was! Dancing around on
six legs, giggling like an idiot child! The little shop clerk,
he says, 'You know, I was going to drown that mutt!
Thought he was useless! Now I see he's got a nose for
game! A born hunter!!' And he laughs like an idiot too!
And I'm laughing harder than ever! But then – he stops
laughing, the little clerk. And I stop laughing too. I turn
round and follow his eyes – to this woman – who's
staring at us! She passes through about fifty shades of
red, curls her lip up! And she trots right out of that
shop, fast as she can! But she stops in the doorway,
turns back, and gives me – a look! Like an animal forced

to look at the mess it's made! Like maybe I'd knocked that little shop clerk down and climbed right up on top of him! And all we'd done was have a good laugh!! So – I knew it was my time to start moving again. Christ knows, this isn't China! Nowhere near! And, like my old dad says, China's hardly even the start for me! See what I mean?

[*She prods the* MAN *again. He utters a long satisfied sigh and begins to snore softly.* MAY *finishes packing and snaps the suitcase shut, singing:*]

'He said to me, on our first night,
He said to me, "I love you!"
He said to me, "Your eyes are bright,
Bright, bright as the stars above you!"'

[*All dressed and packed, she looks down at the sleeping* MAN *for the last time:*]

Thanks so much. I knew you'd be understanding – though plainly broken-hearted! Well, most of you are like that.

[*She smiles, then picks up her suitcase and goes out, singing:*] 'Sing doodle-oodle-oodle-doo,
Sing oodle-doodle-daisy!
Sing doodle-oodle-oodle-doo,
What happened next, dear Maisie?!'

[*She is gone. Her voice fades. Music for the scene change: the first act tune, played by harmonica, concertina and/or piano.*]

Calgary, North West Territories. Spring, 1888. Morning.
Atlantic Avenue, muddy and dusty at the same time.
MAY *comes in with her suitcase. She wears some of the same clothes, but much more soiled and worn now. A dog barks, off.* MAY *stops, takes out a handkerchief, wipes her face and hands.*

MAY [*Sings softly to herself*] 'He said to me, "Your skin is pink,
Your cheeks are satin roses!"
He said to me, and gave a wink,
"Lass, let's at least rub noses!"'

Sing doodle-oodle-oodle-doo,
Sing oodle –"
[*She looks up and stops singing as* VIOLET *comes in,
staggering along the wooden sidewalk. She is no longer
young. Her complexion suggests French-Canadian or
Métis, but her accent is of no fixed origin.*]

VIOLET   Mother of Christ!!
[*She is followed by* SEWARD, *who pushes her, prods her
along the sidewalk. About the same age as* MAY, *he is
dressed all in dark blue; a dark blue cap with some sort
of badge on it.*]

SEWARD   You have somewhere to go? Woman?!

VIOLET   Mother of Christ!
[*They don't see* MAY *at first.*]

SEWARD   Watch your language! This is a public thoroughfare!

VIOLET   Mother of God!

SEWARD   A regular woman wouldn't even know such language,
much less use it! You have somewhere to go?!

VIOLET   Of course! Certainly! I can always go home!

SEWARD   You mean Room Six, over at the Central?

VIOLET   [*Shakes her head 'no'*] Seattle! My mother'll take me in.
She's still quite a young woman herself!

SEWARD   I thought you came from back East somewhere.

VIOLET   [*Laughs*] Who told you that?

SEWARD   You did! Last time I hauled you in! Walk, woman, walk!!
[*He shoves her.*]

VIOLET   I am walking!!

SEWARD   What's wrong? Can't earn your keep anymore? Did they
throw you out?

VIOLET   I earn a better wage than you, Constable! And there's
nobody at the Central sober enough to throw me out!

SEWARD   Walk then! [*He shoves her.*] Walk!!

VIOLET   Mother of Christ –!!
[*They see* MAY. VIOLET *staggers up against a post, tries to
pull herself together.* SEWARD *and* MAY *hold a long, a very
long, look. She smiles and sings, softly, slowly:*]

MAY   'Sing doodle-oodle-oodle-doo –
Sing oodle-doodle-daisy! –"
[SEWARD *grunts, turns on his heel, and goes out quickly,
dusting off his sleeves, then his cap.* VIOLET *stares at* MAY,

who continues watching SEWARD *off, singing:*]
'Sing doodle-oodle-oodle-doo,
What happened next, dear Maisie?'
[*Without taking her eyes off* SEWARD, *who has
disappeared, she speaks in* VIOLET*'s direction:*]
He's a beauty!

VIOLET   Constable Seward? Isn't he just?!
[*She moves to* MAY.]
Thinks he's God, or the Prince of Wales, or somebody!
He acts like he knows you. You must've run into Seward
some place before?

MAY   Oh yes. I run into Constable Seward everywhere.
Practically everywhere I ever was. From the very first.

VIOLET   You're not from around here, are you? How's my colour
look? Awful?

MAY   Mm. How long since you put it on? [*She puts down her
suitcase, sits on the edge of it.*]

VIOLET   Oh, you can't get the really good stuff! Not way the hell
out here! How's my hair look? Awful? [*She sits on the
edge of the suitcase too.*]

MAY   You want some breakfast? I saw a little place down the
street.

VIOLET   Mayo's? Don't eat there! They make a stew by tossing
rotten potatoes into the same ditch water the Chinaman
dumps his suds into! You have anything to drink?
[MAY *takes a small bottle from her coat pocket, offers it
to* VIOLET.]

MAY   I got that from a Baptist deacon in Swift Current. It
tastes like perfume, but it's got less kick.

VIOLET   [*Salutes* MAY *with the bottle.*] Violet Decarmin.

MAY   May Buchanan.
[*They shake hands.*]

VIOLET   Welcome to Calgary! [*She salutes again, drinks, then
hands the bottle back.*] That charming sty I was just
evicted from is called the Hotel Liberty! [*She laughs.* MAY
drinks, then puts the bottle away.] I don't actually live
there! I just like to spread my – my custom around! [*She
laughs.*] Generally I'm over across the river, at the
Central. Favourite flophouse for every saddle tramp that
wanders this far north and west of the Dakotas!

MAY	You think maybe they've got a vacancy?
VIOLET	At the Central? They've got almost nothing but vacancy. Vacancy and me! [*She laughs.*] Are you passing through?
MAY	That's right. Generally.
VIOLET	On your way to where?
MAY	Farther west.
VIOLET	Oh. Smart girl!
MAY	Well – you want to walk me over there? [*She stands.*]
VIOLET	To the Central? I could – [*She stands too.*] – maybe later. The awful thing is – I'm not paid up. They won't let me in. Probably won't even let me onto the verandah! 'Walk, woman, walk!' [*She laughs.*]
MAY	You come on with me. I'll pay you up. [*She picks up her suitcase.*]
VIOLET	It's twelve dollars! Or thereabouts.
MAY	You can give it to me when you get it.
VIOLET	Oh? You must be a rich man's daughter or somebody!
MAY	Rich men's daughters aren't generally moving farther west.
	[*They start down the street.* NETTIE *races in and grabs* VIOLET. *She is very young and frail, and dresses even younger.*]
NETTIE	Violet!!
VIOLET	Mother of Christ!!
NETTIE	Mean woman! Nasty woman!
VIOLET	Hold on now –!
NETTIE	Bad woman!!
VIOLET	Whoa!!
NETTIE	Where were you? I woke up afraid –!
VIOLET	Let go of me!
NETTIE	I thought old Seward had hauled you in again!!
VIOLET	Nettie McDowell –
NETTIE	Where were you?!
VIOLET	Right here at the Liberty! Nettie McDowell –
NETTIE	All night long?!
VIOLET	I'd like you to meet Missus May Buchanan, who is passing through!
	[NETTIE *and* MAY *shake hands.*]
VIOLET	Nettie came in last month. From Saskatchewan. She's not stupid, just slow.

21

NETTIE   Lovely morning!

MAY   Yes, it is.

NETTIE   Look at that sky!

[*They look.* NETTIE *clings to* VIOLET.]

NETTIE   You were at the Liberty all night long?!

VIOLET   Well, see, I was talking with somebody, somebody very nice – and then I fell asleep.

NETTIE   Where're you headed?

VIOLET   The Central.

NETTIE   Oh, they won't let you in! Mister Copithorne says he's not even going to let you onto the verandah!

VIOLET   Missus Buchanan's generously offered to pay me up!

NETTIE   'S that right? You a rich man's daughter or somebody?

VIOLET   Tell us all about yourself!

[*She takes* MAY'*s suitcase and hands it to* NETTIE, *who carries it.* SEWARD *has come back in, at the far end of the street. They don't see him for a moment.*]

MAY   I come from a little place nobody every heard of. Back East. But my more-or-less general direction in life is – or has started to be –

[*She sees* SEWARD *and stops.* VIOLET *and* NETTIE *see him.*]

NETTIE   Oh Jesus!

VIOLET   It's okay, angel! Missus Buchanan knows him. Knows him inside out, backwards and forwards!

NETTIE   'S that right?

[MAY *stares at* SEWARD *another long moment, then begins to sing:*]

MAY   'He said to me, "Your eyes are blue,
As pools both cool and shady ..."
[*She moves on, in* SEWARD'*s direction, followed by* VIOLET *and* NETTIE.] 'He said, "I will be ever true,
And you will be my lady!" ...'
[*They go out, passing very near* SEWARD. *He turns, watches them as they go.*] 'Sing doodle-oodle-oodle-doo –'
[VIOLET *and* NETTIE *join in:*]
'Sing oodle-doodle-daisy!
Sing doodle-oodle-oodle-doo,
What happened next, dear Maisie?'
[*They are gone, laughing. After a moment,* SEWARD *follows*

them out, again brushing his sleeves and cap anxiously.
A dog barks, off. Music for scene change.]

---

*Calgary, North West Territories. Winter, 1888-89.
Morning.*

Parlour of MAY's *house on Edmonton Trail.* NETTIE,
*much better dressed than before, is seated on an
ottoman.* MAY, *also better dressed, stands behind, putting
up* NETTIE's *hair.* VIOLET, *better dressed and coiffed, and a
man named* BABCOCK *(in his fifties, well-dressed) are near
a small wood-burning stove. He is seated, she is standing.
They are listening to* LILY REEVES *sing.* LILY, *originally from
Missouri, a blowzy, bloated woman in her twenties, is in a
large armchair, tucked up with several blankets. She
sings. (The tune from Wallace's* Maritana *is in the Music
Appendix.)*

LILY	'Words cannot scatter The thoughts we fear, For though they flatter, They mock the ear! Hopes will still deceive us With tearful cost, And when they leave us –'
NETTIE	Ouch!
MAY	Sssh!
NETTIE	Don't pull!
LILY	[*Sings at the same time.*] 'The heart is lost! And when they leave us The hea-ea-ea-eaaaaaart –" [*A sort of cadenza.* VIOLET *and* BABCOCK *are impressed.*]
LILY	'– eaaaart – is lost!' [VIOLET *and* NETTIE *applaud.* BABCOCK *yelps his approval, shouts 'Bravo!'*]
VIOLET	Mother of Christ!
LILY	Thank you, thank you.
VIOLET	The sweetest thing I ever heard! Truly is! How about you, Babcock?

BABCOCK	I heard Missus Nordica once in Montreal. Cost me ten bucks too! I'd rather hear Lily any day!
NETTIE	Ten bucks?!
MAY	Hold still, Nettie! We're almost done.
NETTIE	Don't pull.
LILY	I had some strength in my voice a few years back. Before I took sick, started to travel. I was never meant to! Some people aren't meant to ever travel.
MAY	Some aren't meant to ever do anything else. [*She smiles.*]
LILY	[*Shudders.*] Jesus, ain't it cold!
BABCOCK	I had two horses freeze to death already this winter! One of 'em was standing right next to the heat too. I got a big wood-burner down at the stables! You could fit half a dozen of these little black puffers into it! [*He indicates the stove.*] But this old horse was standing there, practically rubbing up against the damned thing! We found him next morning, one half of him still warm as toast! But his other half was froze solid!
VIOLET	[*Hoots.*] Oh, Babcock!
BABCOCK	As God's my witness!
VIOLET	You're full of it!
BABCOCK	Trouble was, you see, he manoeuvred hisself around till it was his left side which was exposed to the cold! It was his left side which froze! Of course, that's where the heart is! His heart was froze!
VIOLET	[*Laughs.*] This gets better and better!
BABCOCK	God's my witness! We cut him open! I took out his heart and held it in my hand, like a big red rock! Till it melted!
VIOLET	Mother of Christ!
MAY	There, Nettie! You look like something out of a picture book!
	[NETTIE *stands, parades around the room.*]
NETTIE	A pretty picture book, May?
MAY	Oh, for certain! One of those real old, real beautiful picture books! With real gold on the pictures. On Sir Lancelot's spurs and in the ladies' hair!
NETTIE	I really do?
	[*A dog barks intermittently, off.*]

MAY	Sit down, Nettie. Lily, sing us another piece. [*She moves to* LILY.] Or maybe you and Mister Babcock are ready to go upstairs for a while? [LILY *looks at* BABCOCK, *tries to smile.*]
BABCOCK	Hell, we can go upstairs anytime! It's not even noon yet!
MAY	You're always the first one here.
BABCOCK	I like to come early, avoid the crowds! [*He laughs.*] And besides, I love to just watch all of you. Together. Putting your hair up. Having breakfast. [*To* LILY.] How about 'Little Peach In An Orchard Grew'?
LILY	I don't know that one anymore. I used to. I used to know all the songs! [*She sniffles.* MAY *takes out a bottle of eau de cologne, rubs some into* LILY's *neck and arms.*]
MAY	Maybe you should go on upstairs. Maybe Mister Babcock can help you remember 'Little Peach' upstairs?
BABCOCK	Hell, what's your rush? There's plenty of time for upstairs! Today Lily feels like singing! Don't you?
LILY	I guess.
MAY	[*To* BABCOCK.] As long as you know you're paying for her time, one way or the other.
BABCOCK	Sing anything, Lily! Anything that'll keep our hearts from freezing solid!
VIOLET	Well, yours wouldn't be any big red rock, Babcock. More like a gum drop, I'd say! [*They laugh.*]
BABCOCK	How 'bout 'Dear Maisie'?! [*Sings hoarsely.*] 'She said to me, "Now lay you down, And I will lie quite near you" –' [*Loud knocking at an exterior door, off.*]
VIOLET	Mother of Christ!
LILY	Who's that?
MAY	Somebody around front.
VIOLET	Who do we know that'd come knocking around front, this time of day? [*She starts out.*]
MAY	Wait! Nettie? You go. [NETTIE *starts out.*] And listen! If he's a stranger to you, just say your mother's not at home right now. You don't expect her before late afternoon.

[NETTIE *pauses a moment, silently repeats this message,
then goes out. More loud knocking, and a dog barking,
off.* VIOLET *looks off, after* NETTIE.]

BABCOCK He's in one hell of a hurry, whoever he is!

VIOLET Could be that cowboy who's always sniffing around
after Nettie! Or that Chinaman with the rat traps!

MAY Go ahead and sing, Lily! Gently –

LILY [*Sings, neither loud nor fast.*]
'He said to me, on our first night,
He said to me, "I love you!"
He said to me, "Your eyes are bright,
Bright, bright as the stars above you!" '
[BABCOCK *joins in, clapping and tapping his foot, trying to
pick up the volume and the tempo.*]
'Sing doodle-oodle-oodle-doo,
Sing oodle-doodle-daisy!'
[MAY *and* VIOLET *are still watching the entrance. The latter
sings along, half-heartedly.*]
"Sing doodle-oodle-oodle-doo,
What happened next, dear Maisie?'
[LILY *starts the second verse alone, somewhat faster and
louder.*] 'He said to me, "Your skin is pink,
Your cheeks are satin roses!" – '
[NETTIE *comes back in, followed by* ROSS. *He is very young,
wears overcoat, boots and hat. Singing is interrupted.*]

LILY Oh! [*She coughs.*]

NETTIE I don't know who it was, May! It was him!
[*She points at* ROSS, *who blushes, takes off his hat.*]

ROSS My name's Ross.

MAY I'm May Buchanan. [*She moves to him. They shake
hands.*] Are you lost, Mister Ross? Snow blind? What can
we do for you?

ROSS I – I heard about you. About all you – ladies –

MAY God! You're shaking like a shot rabbit!
[*All laugh except* ROSS.]

MAY You better go and stand next to the stove!

ROSS Thanks. [*He moves to the stove. A dog barks, off.*]

VIOLET [*To* ROSS.] Stand as close to it as you can bear, precious!
We don't want any of your warm little organs turning
into little red rocks!

[*All laugh except* ROSS. *He blushes, stands with his back to the stove.*]

MAY　New to Calgary, Mister Ross?

ROSS　Yes. Yes, ma'am. From back East.

MAY　Just like me. Passing through? What business are you in?

ROSS　I – oh, I guess I'm looking for work.

MAY　[*Smiles.*] But I expect that's not what you're looking for in my house?

[VIOLET *and* BABCOCK *laugh.*]

ROSS　No, ma'am.

MAY　No. And I expect you still have a little something saved up? Of whatever you brung from back East?

ROSS　A little.

MAY　[*Smiles.*] All right then. That's Violet Decarmin. That's Lily Reeves, who is about to give us a little more music. And that's Nettie, who you met at the door.

[ROSS *nods to each of the women, then looks at* BABCOCK, *waiting for him to be introduced. He isn't.* ROSS *extends his hand.*]

ROSS　Name's Ross.

BABCOCK　So you said! [*He doesn't shake* ROSS*'s hand, but turns to* LILY, *sings, prompting her.*]

'I said to her, "Your eyes are blue
As pools both cool and shady!"'

[LILY *joins in, at* BABCOCK*'s feisty tempo.*]

'I (He) said, "I will be ever true,
And you will be my lady!"'

[BABCOCK *claps and stomps again, forcing* LILY *on, even faster.*]

'Sing doodle-oodle-oodle-doo,
Sing oodle-doodle-daisy!'

[VIOLET *joins in, even louder and faster, and then begins to dance, an impromptu jig or reel.*]

'Sing doodle-oodle-oodle-doo,
What happened next, dear Maisie?!'

[LILY *starts the next verse, somewhat perkier now herself.*]

LILY　'He said to me, "Now lay you down,
And I will lie quite near you!"'

[BABCOCK *and* VIOLET *join in.* ROSS *looks on, still shaking.*
He unbuttons his coat.]
'He (I) said, "Forbear to make a sound,
My mother must not hear you!"'
[MAY *steps forward, dances a few steps with* VIOLET.
BABCOCK *is delighted, whoops.* NETTIE, *who has been*
watching ROSS *constantly, laughs, joins in the singing.*]
'Sing doodle-oodle-oodle-doo,
Sing oodle-doodle-daisy!
Sing doodle –!'
[ROSS *suddenly blurts out, quite loud.*]

ROSS Fact is – I'm in sort of a hurry here!
[*Singing and dancing stop. They all look at him. He*
blushes.]

BABCOCK What'd I tell you? His five bucks is burning a hole in his
pocket! [*He laughs.*] Or something else is!

ROSS [*To* MAY.] Sorry. I – I didn't come here for a concert, you
know. Or a square dance! Sorry.

MAY That's all right, Mister Ross. You want to go upstairs?

ROSS Upstairs?

MAY There's two big rooms upstairs. Each has its own
woodburner. Extra blankets in the cupboard at the end
of the hall, and a bottle of Irish under the washstand.

ROSS Upstairs?

VIOLET [*Grabs his hand.*] Come on, sweetums! I'll show you!

ROSS No! [*He pulls free of* VIOLET, *moves toward* NETTIE.] She
can show me. Miss – Nettie. Can't she?

MAY If you like.

VIOLET Mother of Christ! She can't show you a thing that I can't
show you!

BABCOCK Except a good time!

VIOLET Shut up, Babcock!
[BABCOCK *laughs.* NETTIE *takes* ROSS*'s hand tentatively.*]

NETTIE Come on then. But May's done my hair just like a
picture book. See? You mustn't pull it!

ROSS Oh – wait just a tick?
[*He takes his hand out of* NETTIE*'s, and turns to* MAY. *She*
moves nearer.]

ROSS That'll be how much, Missus Buchanan? I like to keep
these things regular. [*He reaches into his coat.*]

MAY   Depends on how long you stay. But you can ante up
      later. No need to make your mind up right away.
      [BABCOCK *and* VIOLET *exchange a look, titter.*]
ROSS That's all right! My mind's made up! I know exactly
      what I want to –! [*He takes a long-barreled pistol from
      his coat, quickly takes a step or two backwards, and
      trains the gun on the others.*] Stop now! Stop right where
      you are!!
      [BABCOCK *leaps to his feet, starts forward.*]
BABCOCK   For Christ's –! What in hell –!?
ROSS I'm warning you!! [*He points the pistol directly at*
      BABCOCK, *who freezes.*]
BABCOCK   Jesus-Mary-and Joseph!
      [*With the gun still trained on* BABCOCK *and the women,*
      ROSS *half-turns, shouts off, very loud.*]
ROSS Mister Seward?!!
LILY Seward?!
VIOLET   [*At the same time.*] Mother of Christ!
LILY No –!
VIOLET   [*At the same time.*] Not again!!
LILY No!! [*She sniffles.*]
MAY   Hush, Lily!
ROSS Constable Seward, sir!!! [*Turns quickly back to the
      others.*] Missus Buchanan, I am arresting you! For the
      unlicensed purveyance of intoxicants! And for the
      keeping of a disorderly house! The rest of you ladies, for
      being known denizens of the same! And you, Mister
      Babcock, for frequenting of the same! All such acts,
      punishable under the statues and ordinances of –!
      [*Half-turns, shouts desperately.*] Mister Seward!!!
      [*The exterior door is heard, being slammed shut, off.*
      LILY, *weeping, shoves the blankets aside, tries to get out
      of her armchair.*]
LILY Oh no – oh God – I can't –!!
MAY   It's all right, Lily. It'll be all right.
      [LILY *falls back into the chair.* MAY *turns, smiles at* ROSS,
      then shouts off, past him.] Please come in, Constable!
      [SEWARD *comes in, nearly frozen, wearing boots, hat,
      and a voluminous buffalo coat over his police
      uniform.*]

29

ROSS	All secure, Constable! They've been apprised of the charges against them!
SEWARD	Good. That's good. [*He gestures and* ROSS *puts the pistol away.*]
MAY	Make some room for Mister Seward by the stove!
SEWARD	No, thank you. [*He takes off his hat.*]
MAY	But you're shaking! Worse than Lily! Worse than this boy you sent in here to do a man's job! [VIOLET *laughs.*]
ROSS	[*To* MAY.] You just keep quiet, Missus! Mister Seward will do the talking!
MAY	Of course. [*To* SEWARD.] I'm worried about your health. That's all.
SEWARD	It's yourself you ought to worry about! Mister Babcock? You're free to go, sir.
ROSS	But I already said –
BABCOCK	Thank you. [*He puts on his hat and coat.*]
ROSS	I already told him he's charged with frequenting of a –!
SEWARD	Our quarrel's not with the frequenters, Mister Ross. But with these – [*He indicates the women.*] – who make it so frequently and cheaply available. [BABCOCK *starts out.*]
BABCOCK	Thanks, Constable. Cold, isn't it? [*Hesitates.*] February! Ever occur to you it's – a trifle harsh for these ladies –?
SEWARD	Ladies? Better go while you can, Babcock. Supposed to get even colder. [BABCOCK *goes out quickly.*]
NETTIE	[*Faintly.*] Bye-bye!
SEWARD	It's a long walk to the Office of Police, Missus Buchanan. You and your women better wrap up nice and warm.
LILY	[*Sobs.*] We have to – walk?!
MAY	What happened to your wagon, Constable? The one we always have such a good time in?
SEWARD	That's no concern of yours! It's for more important business.
VIOLET	More important to *who*?
SEWARD	I haven't got all day! Move, woman!
MAY	Go on, Violet. Like the Constable says. Upstairs, and get ready.
LILY	Oh God –!

MAY	It'll be all right! [*She smiles at them.*]
VIOLET	Come on, let's bundle you up, Lily! You know you catch any little thing that's going around! Nettie?
	[NETTIE *has been staring at* ROSS, *who blushes.*]
NETTIE	Right here!
	[VIOLET *goes out, shepherding* LILY *and* NETTIE *in front of her.* MAY *calls after them.*]
MAY	Fetch me my scarf and coat! And the doeskin gloves!
SEWARD	Constable Ross?
ROSS	Sir?
SEWARD	This house has a back stairs, I believe. Leading directly down from the second floor? [*He looks at* MAY.]
MAY	That's right.
	[ROSS *stares at them for a moment, then understands.*]
ROSS	Oh yes, sir! Sorry, sir! I'll – I'll stick with them!! [*He hurries out after* VIOLET, LILY *and* NETTIE.]
MAY	They won't make a run for it, Constable. They're faithful.
SEWARD	To the trade?
MAY	To me.
SEWARD	Well, they're women.
MAY	As far as I know. I never had any complaints. [*She laughs, moves closer to him.*] Young Mister Ross is a fine addition to the force. A recent recruit?
SEWARD	That's no concern of yours.
MAY	Are you sure you won't cuddle up to my stove? You're still shaking like a leaf! Real susceptible to the cold, aren't you?
SEWARD	Just keep still. You don't know anything about me.
MAY	Oh now – we've known each other – haven't we? Practically forever. [*She lays her hand on his chest.*]
SEWARD	Take your hand off me.
MAY	I'm admiring your coat. Standard issue? Comes with the job?
SEWARD	I know you, at any rate! You're not fooling anybody. We know about women like you. But most of us – most of them turn a blind eye. Or worse! Take your hands off me!
MAY	But this isn't even properly lined, my God! [*She puts her hand inside his coat.*] You could double-line this. In

David Fox (SEWARD) and Martha Henry (MAY BUCHANAN).

velvet maybe. What they call velvet out here. Wouldn't that feel nice?

SEWARD Goddamn – you –

[*She puts her hand inside his jacket.*]

MAY This jacket's like tissue paper too! Mercury frozen solid inside every thermometer in the Territories, you go around dressed for July!

SEWARD You take your – whore's hands –!

[*She slips her hands inside the waistband of his trousers.*]

MAY If you had a mother, if you had a sister or a wife, she'd look after you better.

SEWARD [*Closes his eyes.*] – off!

32

MAY	But I'm the only woman you've got. [*She continues, moving her hands underneath his clothing.*]
SEWARD	Goddamn –
MAY	Now – for eight and a half cents – I could buy a yard of stuff – just as soft as velvet anyway. Just as sturdy, just as warm ...
SEWARD	May – Buchanan – [*His hands reach out for her throat, then her breast.* ROSS *suddenly comes into the parlour, chattering.*]
ROSS	I'm hurrying them, Constable, but they don't –! [*He stops. He sees what's happening between* MAY *and* SEWARD. SEWARD *opens his eyes, turns, stares at* ROSS *for a moment, then suddenly shoves* MAY *away, roughly. Fastening his clothes, he hurries out of the room.* ROSS *stares at* MAY *for another instant. She smiles at him. He turns and hurried out after* SEWARD.]
ROSS	Constable –?! [*The offstage exterior door is heard, being opened, then slammed shut immediately. A dog barks, off.*]
MAY	[*Sings softly to herself.*] 'Sing-doodle-oodle-oodle-doo, Sing oodle-doodle-daisy!' [VIOLET, *unseen, calls from the stairwell.*]
VIOLET	May?! Come here! Lily just won't stop crying!!
MAY	[*Calls back, not loud.*] Never mind! The wolves are gone! I fed them poison meat!
VIOLET	[*As above, off.*] What'd you say?! [MAY *starts out of the parlour, singing.*]
MAY	'Sing doodle-oodle-oodle-doo, What happened next, dear Maisie?' [*She is gone. Music for scene change.*]

Calgary, North West Territories. Summer, 1889. Afternoon.

The back yard of MAY's *house on Edmonton Trail. Communal laundry is in progress; all of the women, lightly, loosely dressed.* VIOLET *is scrubbing, washing.*

NETTIE *is rinsing, wringing.* MAY *is hanging clothes on a long droopy line.* LILY, *at an upstairs window, sipping a drink, wearing a shawl or kimono, is now seriously unwell.*

MAY [*Sings slowly, freely.*]
'He said to me, on our first night,
He said to me, "I love you!"'
[NETTIE *joins in, harmonizing.*] 'He said to me, "Your eyes are bright,
Bright, bright as the stars above you!"'

LILY [*Sighs.*] Oh, that's a sweet old song!
[VIOLET *skips the refrain, prompts the next verse.*]

VIOLET 'He said to me, "Your skin is pink" –'

LILY I always loved that song!

VIOLET [*and* NETTIE]
'"Your cheeks are satin roses!"'

LILY Always thrilled to it!

VIOLET [*and* NETTIE, MAY]
'He said to me, and gave a wink –'

LILY Before I started to travel!

VIOLET [*and* NETTIE, MAY]
'"Lass, let's at least rub noses!"'
[*They laugh.* NETTIE *hums the refrain underneath.*]

LILY Jesus only knows how long it's been since I felt like singing!

VIOLET [*Calls up to her.*] Not any better today, Lily?

LILY Never going to get any better, I don't guess!

VIOLET Flummery!

LILY It's not flummery! [*She coughs.*]

VIOLET One of Maud Lewis's ladies got real sick last winter. Swelled up with the dropsy, retaining water, just the same as you! But I saw her yesterday, down at the Liberty, lean as a whippet again, dancing like a bride!

LILY Mm. Is she a black lady?

VIOLET What difference does that make?!

LILY Black ladies never die sick! They die old sometimes, but they never die sick!

VIOLET She wasn't black!

LILY But she may have a drop of black blood, way back somewhere, which protects her!

VIOLET	Her name's McKirk, she was born in Glasgow!
LILY	Scottish, huh? Well, they hardly ever die at all!
VIOLET	Mother of Christ!

[MAY *laughs.* LILY *sips. Laundry work continues.*]

MAY 'Sing doodle-oodle-oodle-doo,
Sing oodle-doodle-daisy!'

[THOMAS SHEPHERD *comes in, along the lane behind* MAY's *house. He is in his late twenties, but powerful, already weathered. He weaves a bit as he walks, half-drunk. The women don't see him at first.*]

MAY [*and* NETTIE]
[*Harmonizing as before.*]
'Sing doodle-oodle-oodle-doo,
What happened next, dear Maisie?'

[VIOLET *prompts the next verse.*]

VIOLET 'He said to me, "Your eyes are blue" –'

[MAY *and* NETTIE *join in.* LILY *hums a descant.*]

VIOLET [*and* NETTIE, MAY]
' "As pools both cool and shady!"
He said, "I will be ever true" –'

SHEPHERD [*Sings out loudly.*]
' "And you will be my lady!!" '

[*Startled,* NETTIE *shrieks. They all turn and see him.*]

LILY [*Peering from her window.*] Who's that?

SHEPHERD My favourite song, ladies. My absolute favourite!

[*They look him over.* NETTIE *giggles.*]

NETTIE Lovely afternoon!

SHEPHERD Yes, it is!

LILY Who's that?!

SHEPHERD It certainly is! Not one cloud up there! Not one whisper of a cloud! [*He smiles at* MAY.]

LILY Who's that?!

SHEPHERD And my favourite song, right out of nowhere! What more could a man ask for?

[MAY *moves to him.*]

MAY I'm May Buchanan. [*They shake hands.*]

SHEPHERD Thomas Shepherd.

LILY Who is that?!

MAY [*Calls up to her.*] The man's name is Shepherd, Lily!
[*Turns to* SHEPHERD.] We haven't seen you before.

Jackie Burroughs (VIOLET DECARMIN), Sheila McCarthy
(NETTIE MCDOWELL), Alan Scarfe (THOMAS SHEPHERD),
Barbara Budd (LILY REEVES) and Martha Henry (MAY
BUCHANAN).

SHEPHERD	No, probably not. [*He retains her hand in his.*]
MAY	New around here? Passing through?
SHEPHERD	Depends. My plans just now are changeable, highly changeable.
VIOLET	That's what they all say! [*She laughs, approaches him, extends her hand.*] Violet Decarmin. Welcome to Calgary! [*He smiles at her, hangs onto* MAY.]
SHEPHERD	Thank you. [*To* MAY.] I own some land south of here. On Sheep River. Bought it sight unseen. Saw it for the first time this morning!

VIOLET	South? There's nothing south of here but starving Indians and fat Yankees!
HEPHERD	Well – now there is!
	[MAY *slowly frees her hand from his.*]
MAY	Would you like to come in? Have something to drink?
HEPHERD	I can't.
VIOLET	You got two legs, two lips and a gullet! You can step in for a quick drink!
HEPHERD	I'm buying cattle this afternoon. I ought to try and keep a clear head.
MAY	[*Smiles.*] Maybe you should've considered that a couple of saloons ago!
	[*He laughs.*]
NETTIE	We got coffee! You could have some coffee!
MAY	Leave the man be, ladies! He knows what he wants.
HEPHERD	Yes, I surely do. That's what they always say: 'Old Shepherd at least knows what he wants!' [*Moves close to* MAY, *takes her hand again.*] Might you be in later? To visitors?
MAY	Might be. How much later?
HEPHERD	As soon as I can. After supper?
MAY	All right. Probably. Don't have much more to drink.
	[*She frees herself again. He steps back, grins, tips his hat.*]
HEPHERD	Missus Buchanan.
MAY	Mister Shepherd.
HEPHERD	Ladies! [*He tips his hat to the others, and goes out, weaving, singing.*]

'I said to her, "Now lay you down,
And I will lie quite near you!"
I said, "Forbear to make a sound,
My mother must not hear you!" '
[*Laughing, he disappears.* MAY *turns, looks at* VIOLET, NETTIE *and* LILY, *all of whom are staring at her expectantly. She frowns and goes back to work, hanging up clothes. The others exchange looks and titter.* NETTIE *goes back to the wringer.* VIOLET *stares after* SHEPHERD. LILY *leaves the window for a moment, returns with a fresh drink which she sips and dabs on her forehead.*]

37

MAY [*As she goes back to work.*]
'Sing doodle-oodle-oodle-doo,
Sing oodle-doodle-daisy!'

NETTIE Thomas – that's a good name!

MAY 'Sing doodle-oodle-oodle–do –'

NETTIE A good man's name!

VIOLET [*Loud.*]
'What happened next, dear Maisie?!'
[*She and* MAY *exchange a look.* VIOLET *laughs.* NETTIE
leaves the wringer, stares off after SHEPHERD *too.* LILY *also
looks off, in that direction. They are all looking that way.*]

NETTIE He's from back East too, I guess. Has eyes just like yours,
May. Those eyes that can total you up, know you inside
and out in half a minute! From back East, probably
sweated in some factory for every nickel he's got! Now
he's come out west, to find land and cattle. And the
right woman before he's too old. Rarely touches the
booze, I bet. Only today he got a little careless!
[*She turns, looks at* MAY. LILY *laughs, coughs.*]

LILY He's come from up North. Got that nasty spark in his
eye that they always got, when they broke themselves
for gold and never found any! He's fed up, worn out, and
mean as two weasels! Nothing for him to plant a claim
on now but some woman – God help her! He swears
and fornicates, and believes with his fists now that his
heart's broke! And when a woman gets 'a little careless,'
she's called a damned drunk!
[*She looks at* MAY. VIOLET *suddenly laughs sharply,
sarcastically.*]

VIOLET He's a Yank. A Yank who's done time for stealing – I
don't know what – something of no real value!
Something bright or silly that took his eye. Now he's
come up North to try and hide from all that! He's one of
them that never really grows up! Still falls down taking
off his own trousers! He's a bloody Yank, yes, 'cause they
all show their teeth when they smile, like a set of loaded
dice! Chances are, we'll never see him again. From
south of the line, they all get blind drunk on two glasses
of watered beer! [*Sings, imitating* SHEPHERD.]
'"And you will be my lady!!"'

[NETTIE *and* LILY *laugh.* VIOLET *turns, looks at* MAY. *They are all looking at her. She turns away, finishes hanging up the wet clothes.*]

MAY   He's a man. A man with feet and legs and a backside and privates and a belly and a chest and shoulders and a neck and a head with hair on top of it and nothing of much concern to me inside it!

[*The others titter. She turns, looks at all of them.*]

Thomas Shepherd of Sheep River! That's not the sort of kindling to start fires under me. I've got to travel farther, much farther, before I find anybody – anything that'll start any fires in me!

[*The others grin, exchange looks, laugh.*]

VIOLET   Crackle, crackle.

LILY   Spark, spark.

NETTIE   Flicker, flicker!

[*They laugh louder.* MAY *dismisses them with a gesture and starts out.*]

VIOLET   Crackle, crackle!

LILY   Spark, spark!

NETTIE   Flicker, flicker!!

[MAY *hurries out, as though pursued.* VIOLET *and* NETTIE *run out after her, and* LILY *disappears from the upstairs window, all shouting, singing, ad lib, over and over.*]

VIOLET   Crackle, crackle!!

LILY   Spark, spark!!

NETTIE   Flicker, flicker!!

[*They are gone, their voices fade. Music for scene change.*]

Nose Creek, near Calgary, North West Territories. Autumn, 1890. Evening.

The prairie, which a meandering creek has turned at places into marsh. A large but shallow slough at one side. A few hills, the low banks of the creek, grass.

SEWARD comes in, followed by ROSS, *both in uniform.* SEWARD *dusts his sleeves and cap. A dog barks, far off, intermittently.* SEWARD *and* ROSS *look around, then crouch.*

SEWARD	'So he carried me away in the spirit into the wilderness: and I saw a woman sit upon a scarlet coloured beast, full of names of blasphemy, having seven heads and ten horns.'
ROSS	Sir?
SEWARD	This is it. The place they always come to.
ROSS	Yes, sir. It's nice out here by the creek.
SEWARD	It's wet and cool. It's quiet. They come out here when it's too hot, inside her house. It stayed hot this year.
ROSS	It did, yes, sir.
SEWARD	Stay close to me. Don't move around much. They'll come along any time now.
	[*They sit and wait on the bank of the creek.*]
SEWARD	'And the woman was arrayed in purple and scarlet colour, and decked with gold and precious stones and pearls, having a golden cup in her hands full of abominations and filthiness of her fornications.'
ROSS	That's the Bible. Isn't it?
SEWARD	Revelation of Saint John.
ROSS	Sir?
SEWARD	[*Looks at him.*] The Beloved Disciple.
ROSS	Yes, sir. [*He rises to a crouch, stares around.*]
SEWARD	We'll hear them coming, Mister Ross. Long before they get here. We'll hear them laugh and snort and whinny. No regular woman makes all that noise!
	[ROSS *looks at him, sits beside him again.*]
	Time's passed, Mister Ross. A few months. She thinks I'm not watching anymore. She thinks I don't see her! [*Not loud but fierce.*] I see, May Buchanan! I see right through you! I lift the skin right off you with my eyes! I always could! I see your filthy past. I see your filthy present. I see your future! Your painted corpse, beginning to melt and smear! In a casket of rotted French silk! Enticing the worms! Awakening the desire of maggots, darling May!!
	[*He smiles.* ROSS *stares at him. A dog barks, farther and farther away.* SEWARD *rises to a crouch, stares around.*]
ROSS	You've known her a long time, I guess.
SEWARD	What? Who?
ROSS	Missus Buchanan.

SEWARD	Who told you so?
ROSS	I don't know. I heard that. I heard people saying so. She says so, doesn't she? I think you told me so once.
SEWARD	I've known her? I knew her, first time I set eyes on her. Before that! I know enough to judge anyway. I have judgement. I know the laws which apply, God's and man's. Their sex was put upon this earth to demonstrate to ours the divine aspiration! But these aren't regular women, Mister Ross. They have betrayed their purpose! Upset the balance of Creation! – Where are they? [*He sits beside* ROSS *again, reaches inside the tunic of his uniform, and slowly takes out a shapeless female undergarment, soft, loose.*] Look at this.
ROSS	Sir? [*He takes it from* SEWARD.] What is it?
SEWARD	French silk is what it is. You know how hard she has to work, what sort of profit she has to turn? To get French silk?
ROSS	[*Looks at it.*] French silk.
	[SEWARD *shoves the garment toward* ROSS*'s face.*]
SEWARD	The stench of them! All the same! Can you smell it? Can you smell it without being sick? Sick inside and out? [ROSS *hands the garment back to* SEWARD, *who tucks it inside his tunic again.*] 'And upon her forehead was a name written, MYSTERY, BABYLON THE GREAT, THE MOTHER OF HARLOTS AND ABOMINATIONS OF THE EARTH.'
ROSS	I never realized you were – You're a religious man, Constable.
SEWARD	It's not religion, Mister Ross! 'Religion' is for children! And Catholics. Passion, Mister Ross. Not what they call passion out here, their filth, their money and French silk! Pure passion. The passion to know and to judge. The life. The passion. The death. The resurrection, to life or to the fire! Understand, Mister Ross? 'Religion' is easy, painless. It takes the strength of an angel to wrestle with passion. One's own. Above all, one's own. [NETTIE *is heard singing, unseen, considerably in the distance.*]
NETTIE	'Sing doodle-oodle-oodle-doo, Sing oodle-doodle-daisy!'

41

[SEWARD *and* ROSS *rise to a crouch, peer across the prairie.*]

NETTIE [*and* MAY]

[*Off, harmonizing.*]

'Sing doodle-oodle-oodle-doo,

What happened next, dear Maisie?!'

[*Laughter, humming, ad lib conversation, off, drawing nearer.* SEWARD *gestures to* ROSS, *and they both quickly scuttle off across the prairie, disappearing in the tall grass along the river bank.* MAY *is heard singing, drawing nearer.*]

MAY 'He said to me, "It is my will

To close your mouth with kisses!"

He said, "My babes are sleeping still" –'

[VIOLET, *also unseen, joins in, hooting.*]

MAY [*and* VIOLET]

' "And please don't wake my missus!!" '

[*Laughter, off. A dog barks, very far away, almost inaudible. After a moment,* MAY, VIOLET, NETTIE, LILY, SHEPHERD *and* BABCOCK *come in. They have all been drinking. The women are barefoot.* SHEPHERD *is holding* MAY*'s hand, though they walk quite far apart.* BABCOCK *and* NETTIE *both have their arms around* LILY; *they support her as she plods along, very ill.* VIOLET *has tucked her skirts up, and is wading through the marshy water at the edge of the creek. They all sing, a considerable lusty cacophony.*]

MAY [*and* VIOLET, NETTIE, LILY, SHEPHERD, BABCOCK]

'Sing doodle-oodle-oodle-doo,

Sing oodle-doodle-daisy!

Sing doodle-oodle-oodle-doo,

What happened next, dear Maisie?!'

[SHEPHERD *starts up the first verse again.*]

SHEPHERD 'I said to her, on our first night,

I said to her, "I love you!" '

[BABCOCK *joins in this masculine version of the verse.*]

SHEPHERD [*and* BABCOCK]

'I said to her, "Your eyes are bright" -'

[VIOLET *suddenly shrieks.*]

VIOLET Aaaaagghh!!!! [*Runs up onto the muddy bank, raising her*

skirts even higher, and vigorously clawing at her legs.]
Aaaagh!!!

NETTIE Violet?!

LILY [*At the same time.*] What is it?!!

BABCOCK [*At the same time.*] Jesus Christ, what now?!
[VIOLET *stops shrieking, studies her bare legs for a moment, then suddenly shrieks and claws again.*]

VIOLET Aaaaagghh!!!!

NETTIE Stop that!!

MAY [*At the same time.*] Violet?!

VIOLET Bloodsuckers!!

BABCOCK What in hell –?!

VIOLET Bloodsuckers, fleshcrawlers, waterdancers!! This water – this creek is full of 'em!! [*She brushes and slaps her legs loudly.*]

BABCOCK Your head is full of 'em!!
[*All laugh except* VIOLET.]

VIOLET Go ahead! You can laugh! One of Carrie Hough's ladies was splashing around in one of these sloughs last month – while a bevy of her regulars stood around enjoying the spectacle! Next morning, they found her stretched out on the bank, white as Kerry linen! Parasites as big as Babcock's cigar, crawling all over her extremities!!
[*The others laugh.*]
As God's my witness!
[*Laughter.*]

BABCOCK One of these days, Violet, God is going to drop a blanket over your cage, permanently!
[*Laughter.*]

VIOLET Mother of Christ! There are none so blind as those that –

BABCOCK As those that stay out after dark! We should be starting back. I'm ready to start back! Everybody ready to start back?

NETTIE I'm not! I'm never going to be ready! Look at that sky!!
[*She and* BABCOCK *help* LILY *to sit and rest a moment on a grassy elevation.*]

BABCOCK Whoa, listen! Ring dove!
[*They listen.*]

LILY	[*Softly.*] Jesus only knows how long it's been since I felt like splashing around!
BABCOCK	[*Disappointed.*] No. Hermit thrush!
SHEPHERD	[*As* MAY *drops his hand, moves away.*] Look at that sky, May! You could sit right on top of the Rocky Mountains, and you wouldn't feel one bit closer to it! It's here. It's right on top of us! [*He takes a bottle of whiskey from his pocket, drinks, passes it around.*] Not a cloud in sight! But anywhere you point a finger up there – the air – the air itself is different colours! See what I mean? Orange. Yellow. Blue. Violet!
VIOLET	[*Brushes her legs, turns to him.*] What?!
	[SHEPHERD, MAY *and* BABCOCK *laugh.*]
VIOLET	[*To* SHEPHERD.] What did you want?
SHEPHERD	Nothing.
VIOLET	Mother of Christ! [*She scratches her legs through her skirts.*]
MAY	Pay him no mind, Violet. He's just drunk.
SHEPHERD	[*Moves close to her again.*] I'm not, you know. I'm just – poetical.
MAY	Yes, well, I knew you were something.
VIOLET	Get up, Lily! It's filthy out here. You're filthy! We're not staying!
LILY	I'm not so sure – I can walk!
VIOLET	Well, nobody's going to tote you! You're too fat!
LILY	It's not my fault! Jesus!
	[BABCOCK *and* VIOLET *help her to her feet.*]
VIOLET	Nettie?
NETTIE	Right here!
VIOLET	Get out of that mud! There's a kind of bloodsucker that specializes in mud! Don't you know anything?! There's a kind of fleshcrawler that won't live anywhere except in mud! [*She brushes* NETTIE*'s legs.*]
MAY	Sounds like a certain police constable that we all know and love!
	[*They all laugh, except* VIOLET.]
VIOLET	Come on, everybody! We're going! Nettie?
NETTIE	Right here!
	[*They start out,* VIOLET *and* BABCOCK *now supporting* LILY;

NETTIE, *following behind, twirling in slow circles along the creek bank.*]

LILY My mother passed out of her mortal existence in just this fashion!

BABCOCK Strolling home from a picnic? [*He laughs.*]

VIOLET Shut up, Babcock.

LILY First, her rosy colour went, and she began to put on weight. Her fingers refused to function, and her shoulder, then her entire right arm seized up! Her eyes grew a milky layer of skin, through which she saw only shapes and a few bright colours. She never ate! She never slept!

BABCOCK But was she happy otherwise? [*He laughs.*]

VIOLET Shut up, Babcock!

 [*The four of them continue off, slowly, at* LILY'*s pace.* MAY *starts to follow them.* SHEPHERD *takes her hand again. Far away, a dog barks again intermittently.*]

SHEPHERD Let's stay a while?

MAY It's dark.

SHEPHERD Not real dark. Not for an hour yet.

 [VIOLET, *no longer seen, calls.*]

VIOLET Missus Buchanan?!

MAY [*To* SHEPHERD.] We'll get cold.

SHEPHERD No, we won't. I won't let us! [MAY *drops his hand again, but calls off.*]

MAY Go on ahead! Don't wait for us!

VIOLET [*Off, calls.*] It's a half hour walk back to town!

MAY [*Calls.*] You're not my mother, Violet!

BABCOCK [*Unseen, but loud.*] Even if you are old enough!

VIOLET [*Off, shouts.*] Shut up, Babcock!!

 [NETTIE, *likewise unseen, is heard singing. Her voice grows fainter and fainter.*]

NETTIE 'He said to me, "Your eyes are blue
  As pools both cools and shady!"'
 [MAY *wanders to the edge of the slough, stares into it.*]

NETTIE [*Off.*]
 'He said, "I will be ever true,
  And you will be my lady!"'

[*The dog barks, off.* SHEPHERD *approaches* MAY, *embraces her from behind, drinks from his whiskey bottle.*]

SHEPHERD My grandmother was part Indian. Cherokee. Told us our fortunes by gazing into a pool of water. Nine times out of ten she was right too! What do you see in there, May? [*She moves away from him again.*]

MAY I'm not part Indian.

SHEPHERD What do you see?

MAY [*Troubling the water with her foot.*] Troubles.

SHEPHERD For who?

MAY For you, of course.

SHEPHERD What kind of troubles?

MAY May Buchanan troubles.

SHEPHERD Anybody ever die of that, I wonder?

MAY They didn't actually die maybe. Some of them got very sick.

SHEPHERD Wasted away? Never ate? Never slept?

MAY That's right. For a while. Then they found their appetite again, somewhere else.

SHEPHERD Well, I'm glad to know you're not usually fatal! [*He laughs, drinks, moves near again, grabs her.*]

MAY [*Laughs.*] Let go of me!
[*They struggle playfully.*]

SHEPHERD What about you? What's the water got to say about you?

MAY Oh – it likes me. [*She frees herself and wades into the shallow slough.*] It likes me!

SHEPHERD May? Come back here! You're still angry, aren't you? About yesterday?

MAY I don't get angry with a fool!

SHEPHERD I wasn't fooling!

MAY Asking me to sell my house? To cut free from my ladies and move in with you? Marry you! You're either a fool or a lunatic. Which is it?

SHEPHERD Which would you prefer?

MAY I prefer my own kind of pleasure, my own kind of peace – and my own pennies to anybody else's dimes!

SHEPHERD That's no answer! [*He finishes off the whiskey, and tosses the empty bottle into the slough near* MAY. *It splashes her.*] Come here! [*He wades in after her.*]

MAY [*Wading farther.*] If I was to sell up and move on, it

wouldn't be south – to Sheep River – to lawfully warm my feet against you, Thomas Shepherd. It'd be farther west!

SHEPHERD [*Wading farther after her.*] West? How come? What's out there?

MAY No rules, no laws, no judges.

SHEPHERD [*Grabs her.*] I love you, May!

MAY According to my dear old dad!
[*They struggle, less playfully now.*]

MAY Let go of me!

SHEPHERD I love you!

MAY You're drunk. You're crazy!

SHEPHERD Babcock says I am! He says you're as near as he's ever seen to a confirmed, guaranteed-for-life, dyed-in-the-wool whore!

MAY Babcock's a smart man!
[*She frees herself again, moves toward the bank of the slough.* SHEPHERD *follows her, splashing around desperately.*]

SHEPHERD Jesus, I love you! I know what you were, what you are! And goddamn you, goddamn them all, I love you anyway! I want you anyway!!

MAY Well? You've got me!

SHEPHERD No! Not enough of you! Not a bigger share than anybody else has got!
[*He grabs her by her wet clothing. She tries to push him away. They fall together onto the muddy slough bank.*]

SHEPHERD It's months now! Christ, it's how many months?! It's more than a year! You never let me get close! Not closer than anybody else!
[MAY *tries to pull free, to stand. He holds her close and fast.*]

SHEPHERD Listen to me! Tell me! What is it you're so unwilling to part with?! The fat men, the fast money, the friendly ladies?!

MAY Myself!

SHEPHERD You've got nothing, May! Nothing that'll last!

MAY Myself!

SHEPHERD You've got the town fathers and mothers, priests, preachers, and every less successful madam within two

	hundred miles breathing down your neck! Waiting for you to break one law too many! For you to get old or fat or sick!
MAY	And what would I have with you, Thomas Shepherd?
SHEPHERD	You'd have me!
MAY	I don't know what that is! [*She manages to free herself, and walks or crawls up onto the drier prairie.*] I'm never going to know what that is!! [SHEPHERD *crawls after her.*]
SHEPHERD	You got Constable Seward, sniffing around! Taking notes every time you laugh or take a bath or blink your eyes! [*He catches at her skirt. She pulls it violently out of his grasp.*] *He* scares you, doesn't he?!
MAY	Seward? He doesn't scare me! I don't know what scares me! Having to be still scares me. Having to lie down and just be still! [SHEPHERD *reaches for her again. She crawls or walks quickly away.*] I've known Seward practically forever! He's not half the trouble to me that you are!
SHEPHERD	I love you, May!! [*He sits up in the mud, stares at her. She is still, staring back.*] I love you. How can you look at me and see nothing but troubles?
MAY	I look at you ... I look at you, and I see rich old Mister Leslie when I was fourteen. I see that hamfisted boy from Berlin. Not one bit of difference between one of you and the next! Nothing I can really see, really feel! I see Jim Stephens from the Farmers' Bank, who licks twenty-dollar bills and pastes them to my breasts, every Tuesday afternoon! Everything, everyone can be washed away with a little soap, dried away with a little towel, rinsed away with a mouthful of Irish. You're no different, Thomas Shepherd. It all gets washed away. Except myself.
SHEPHERD	Goddamn it, May – I want to – understand you – [*He crawls to her. She is still.*]
MAY	Myself. That'll last. That'll stick. Whether I want it or not! I can't cut free from that! Not here! Not in the far Pacific or in China! But – farther on – out there –

SHEPHERD   I want – close – I want closer –! [*He puts his arms around her and slowly lays her back on the prairie. She doesn't resist.*]

MAY   There's nothing really close. Nothing that's part of us. Can't be. Nothing really solid and stuck. Except myself. The rest of it is all water, all things soft and common and changeable as water. Always. The booze, the sweat, the vomit, the piss, the blood, the seed, flowing out of us and onto each other, and then right off of us, and onto the earth, like water, a little water, a little wet –
[SHEPHERD *wraps one of his legs around both of hers. He moves half on top of her, kissing her neck, arms and breasts.*]
– onto the earth, onto her dirty skin! And then the sky, the coloured air breathes it in, sucks it up, gathers it into steam and clouds! And clouds that spray and sweat and bleed and flow down onto us, and seep into us again, again, again, again, again.
[SHEPHERD *is now very excited, making love to her, not listening.*]
The falling onto us, seeping into us, and then the flowing out of us again – is all there is! Except myself!

SHEPHERD   Yourself!

MAY   Myself!

SHEPHERD   Yourself!!

MAY   This! Myself!! And somewhere – far – somewhere far out there – this! – myself!! – melts too – flows out of me too – can be washed and dried away – myself too! A little water! And it flows away!!
[SHEPHERD *has started to lift* MAY's *skirts, and to position himself between her legs. She does not resist. Suddenly he grows still, his eye caught by something in the distance, in the twilight.*]

SHEPHERD   – May –?

MAY   What? This!

SHEPHERD   Be still, May! Wait –?

MAY   What is it? Nothing.

SHEPHERD   Sshhh!
[*He slides away from her, still staring. In the distance,* SEWARD *and* ROSS *can be dimly seen, slouching through*]

the twilight toward them. SHEPHERD *strains to see into the darkness.*]

Shit –!

MAY   Shepherd –?

SHEPHERD   Son of a bitch!!

[*He gets to his feet.* SEWARD *and* ROSS, *seen only as dark grey shapes, realize they've been seen and involuntarily retreat a few steps.*]

MAY   Where – what are you doing? Shepherd?!

[SEWARD *suddenly cries out, very strong, from a considerable distance.*]

SEWARD   Missus Buchanan?!

[SHEPHERD *takes a few steps in* SEWARD*'s direction, stumbling, shouts back.*]

SHEPHERD   You! Get the bloody hell out of here!!

[*He turns back, helps* MAY *to her feet. At the same time,* SEWARD *and* ROSS *move a bit nearer, become a bit more visible.*]

SEWARD   May Buchanan! Having observed your activities for some considerable time now–!

SHEPHERD   [*Turns, moves toward him again.*] You shit!!

SEWARD   [*Oblivious of* SHEPHERD*'s approach.*] It is my duty to place you under arrest and to charge you with gross public indecency, Mister Ross here as witness!! I shall ask the circuit judge to exercise clemency in granting you forty-eight hours in which to quit the township forever!!

SHEPHERD   You filth!!

ROSS   Look out, Mister Seward!!

SHEPHERD   You shit!!

[*He hurls himself through the darkness toward* SEWARD, *judging direction more by sound than by sight. He lands on* ROSS *first.* ROSS *cries out, tries to get to his feet, but* SHEPHERD *weighs him down.* SEWARD *moves toward the slough, stares at* MAY *from a distance of several feet. She stares back at him for a moment.*]

SEWARD   May Buchanan.

ROSS   [*Screams.*] Mister Seward!!

[*Pinned to the ground,* ROSS *manages to get his revolver out of its holster, but* SHEPHERD *knocks it out of his hand. It is lost in the darkness.*]

SHEPHERD You scum!!

ROSS Con – stable?!!!

[*They continue to struggle in the dirt.* SEWARD *stares at* MAY. *She suddenly turns, moves away to the slough, washes her feet and legs in the turgid water. At the same time,* ROSS *finally succeeds in escaping from* SHEPHERD. *Running for his life, he brushes past* SEWARD *in the darkness.*]

SEWARD Constable Ross?!! You will stand your ground!! You will not allow this whore, this Babylon –!!

[*His command turns to a cry as* SHEPHERD *tackles him from behind. They roll across the grass and mud together.* ROSS *disappears into darkness.* SHEPHERD *is on top of* SEWARD *now, hammering him with both fists.* SEWARD *does not resist, does not attempt to reach his revolver.*]

SHEPHERD You scum! You filth!! You shit!!!

[*He gasps, but continues pounding* SEWARD. *At a considerable distance, a dog barks, and a locomotive whistles mournfully.* MAY *finishes washing herself, moves toward the two men.*]

MAY Shepherd?!

SHEPHERD You – filth!!

MAY Stop now! Shepherd!!

[*After several more blows to* SEWARD*'s face,* SHEPHERD *sags, exhausted, and slumps forward, still on top of* SEWARD. *The latter does not move or make a sound.*]

MAY Come here. Come over here!

[*Winded,* SHEPHERD *stands, staggers in* MAY*'s general direction.*] This way. That's it! Easy, over here!

[SHEPHERD *finds her, and sags against her. They stumble together, then find their balance.*] Did you kill him?

[*The whistle of the locomotive again, considerably nearer. The tracks, although not visible, must pass quite near the creek and slough.*]

SHEPHERD No – I – I tried to!

MAY We better clear out of here! Can you walk? That kid'll be back in Calgary, saying he was ambushed by a whole herd of whores and their Cherokee lovers!! [*She laughs.*]

SHEPHERD [*Still clinging to her.*] Better – clear out!

MAY   Violet'll close the house down! I can't afford to be seen
in town for a few weeks! Months maybe!
*[Whistle of the locomotive, still nearer. Dim smoky rays,
from the incandescent lamp on its engine, spread across
the prairie and the creek.]*
Come on! We'll go to your place!
[They start out, MAY *supporting him, her arms wrapped
around him.]*

SHEPHERD   My place –!
*[Music, underscoring: the first act tune, played on
harmonica, concertina, and piano. It crescendos to the
end of the scene.]*

MAY   *[As they struggle along.]* I'll pack up a few things! We'll
get into your wagon! I'll put both arms around you like
this, and I'll leave them there till we get to Sheep River!!
*[*SHEPHERD, *exhausted, tries to laugh.]*

SHEPHERD   Jesus, I – I won you! I won you, May Buchanan! I won
you!!
*[Locomotive whistle and lights draw quickly nearer,
brighter, illuminating more of the wet grassy expanse.]*

MAY   Pick up your hat! Come on. Hurry!
*[*SHEPHERD *picks up his hat, which is near* SEWARD's
motionless form. MAY *and* SHEPHERD *look at the constable
for a moment, then step around or over him.* SHEPHERD
leans against MAY *again, as they make their way off,
quickly disappearing along the creek bank, the direction
from which they entered.]*
*[Locomotive, very noisy and smoky, rattles nearer still.
Together with the music, it becomes almost deafening.]*
*[*SEWARD, *bloody and shaking, raises himself from the
dust and crushed grass. The lights of the locomotive
wash over him. He squints, grins, into the lights.]*
*[The locomotive is now so near, so loud, it's surely about
to appear at any moment.* SEWARD *trembles, grins.]*
[Sudden darkness and silence.]

INTERVAL

Sheep River, North West Territories. Summer, 1891.
Afternoon.

    A narrow bed. MAY, *in her late thirties, is lying there*
with THOMAS SHEPHERD. *She wears a flimsy cotton shift. He*
is naked. Both are awake; it is paralyzingly hot.

    Music: the second act tune, 'The Bluest Eyes,' played
slowly, disjointedly on harmonica, concertina or piano.
(See Music Appendix.)

SHEPHERD	... May?
MAY	... Mm?
SHEPHERD	It's hot.
MAY	It's so still ... I'm suffocating.
	[*He reaches out, touches her.*] Don't. I have to lie still – try to remember how to breathe.
SHEPHERD	Might help – if you took your shimmy off.
MAY	Take it off, and put you on? No, thanks.
SHEPHERD	You're shiny. You're beautiful. [*He touches her.*]
MAY	Don't!
	[*Pause.*]
SHEPHERD	We'll get out then – go for a walk? Down along the river. You can lie down in the sand. I'll pour handfuls of fresh cold water over you. Later on, we'll make a fire...? How about a bedtime story then?

[*She doesn't look at him.*]
Back in Colorado Springs where I grew up –
[*She turns her back to him.*] Listen, I never told anybody
about this before!
[*He moves closer to her, without touching her, and tells*
his story softly.]
Back in Colorado Springs, there was a rich woman.
There were lots of rich women, all of them 'gold mine
widows.' But there was one in particular – my mother
kept house for her for a while. Everyone said my rich
woman was over sixty. I don't know. I was seventeen at
the time. She was real old. She asked me to do some
errands for her. Later on, to do some yard work. Later
on, to do some work inside her house. [*Laughs.*] Christ, I
didn't know what was happening! I mean, she wasn't

Martha Henry (MAY BUCHANAN) and Alan Scarfe (THOMAS SHEPHERD).

exactly the first, but she might as well have been! She was the first one that really gave a damn, let me get closer than – I liked her! I liked her house. Jesus knows it was better, cleaner than the one I came from!

MAY   [*Doesn't move.*] And she – paid you?

SHEPHERD   ... Sometimes.

[MAY *turns, looks at him, and laughs.*]

I never asked her to pay for that!

MAY   But you kept her money, just the same!

SHEPHERD   Damned right!

[MAY *laughs louder.* SHEPHERD *laughs too. He touches her lightly, she doesn't resist.*]

I never told anybody! But of course, they all knew! I think my mother knew, but she never said anything. It went on for five or six months. My rich woman, I guess her hair must've been white underneath. But she dyed it red, a brilliant red, geranium red! I'd run into somebody on the street or in the bar, and he'd pick something off my collar or my sleeve. 'What's this, young Tom?!' Looks

54

like a long, long red, brilliant red hair!! Now where'd that come from, I wonder?!'
[*They laugh together again. He kisses her lightly.*]
But I didn't give a damn! I had a little pocket money for the first time in my life! And I knew exactly what I wanted to do with it! Buy something new, something untried, unbroken, something of my own. To the east there was only dirt farmers, scratching for corn and peas. To the west there was early death, scratched out of gold or silver. In the south, everything was dead, dead for years! So I came north. I found you!
[*He kisses her. Starts to put an arm or leg around her. She moves away.*]

MAY   You found me! Neither new nor untried nor unbroken.
[*She laughs.*]

SHEPHERD   Maybe not. Still – it's something of my own!
[*He reaches for her again. She stands, moves away.*]
Where're you going?

MAY   I'm suffocating? [*She takes a light cotton robe from the foot of the bed, wraps it around herself.*]

SHEPHERD   And you're putting on more clothes? May? Come back. I'll shut up!

MAY   [*Turns to him.*] No, you won't! You haven't shut up for half a minute for nearly a year now! Even when you're asleep – when we're both asleep – I hear you talking: 'Don't, May. Don't go back. Don't go back to your house, to your men, to your ladies, to your life!' [*She suddenly stoops and takes her small suitcase from under the bed.*]

SHEPHERD   [*Sits up.*] May?!

MAY   I'm going!

SHEPHERD   Back to Calgary? You figure you've laid low for long enough?

MAY   I've laid low for a hundred years. Longer! [*She begins collecting clothes from the bedstead, packing them into the suitcase.*]

SHEPHERD   May? Don't! [*He gets out of bed, puts on trousers.*]

MAY   But I'm through with bloody Calgary! Presbyterians and horsepiss! Rules, laws and judges! 'Walk, woman, walk!' Let Violet light up the Hotel Liberty! Let little Nettie and my sweet wilting Lily dodge the constables, enflame

cowpokes and tinware salesmen! You never let me keep
an eye on my ladies anyway! I'm headed elsewhere!

SHEPHERD   Farther west? [*He watches her pack for a moment, then
suddenly seizes the suitcase, throws it down on the floor,
spilling most of its contents.*] You're not going!! I'm not
letting you!!
[MAY *looks at him, very still.*]

MAY   ... You're not? [*She sits on the edge of the bed, smiles at
him.*] So you want to – what? Talk some more? [*She
laughs.*]

SHEPHERD   Talk or shut up. Go for a walk or lie still. [*Moves near
her.*] Love each other or don't touch! Whatever you like!
But you're not going!

MAY   Whatever I like?

SHEPHERD   You're not ever going.
[MAY *stares at him for another long moment, then
reaches out, unbuttons the top two buttons of his
trousers.*]
May...?
[*She gently pulls him nearer. He leans into her, and they
kiss. After the kiss,* MAY *lies back on the narrow bed. He
crawls over her, kissing her, and starts again to wrap
himself around her. But* MAY *has reached under her
pillow and has taken out a small short-barreled pistol.
She pokes it into the centre of* SHEPHERD's *bare chest. He
scoots away from her slightly, sees the pistol, and doesn't
move. He looks at her.*]

MAY   My valise, Mister Shepherd. Pick it up, please. Put it on
this bed.
[*She trains the pistol on him steadily. He stares at her.
After a moment, he stands abruptly, and stoops for the
suitcase. At the same time,* MAY *gets out of bed, wraps the
cotton robe around herself tightly with one hand, never
taking the pistol off* SHEPHERD. *He slams the suitcase
down on the bed viciously, then looks at* MAY *again. She
smiles.*]
Now pack my things. All my things, please.
[*After another long moment,* SHEPHERD *turns, retrieves*
MAY's *clothes from the floor and begins shoving them
angrily into the suitcase.* MAY *watches him, perhaps*

directs the packing with gestures of the gun. Smiling,
she sings softly.]
'The bluest eyes,
So wise,
And yellow hair,
So fair,
The dearest heart,
And more:
Did he get what he came for?'
[SHEPHERD *locates a few more articles of clothing, shoes,
stockings, etc., from under or near the bed, and packs
these too, glaring at* MAY *from time to time. She watches
him, sings.*]
'The shelt'ring arm,
So warm,
The proudest gaze,
Ablaze,
The lips that all –'
[SHEPHERD, *who has moved closer to* MAY, *as though to
close the suitcase, suddenly hurls a heavy article of
clothing at her, turning the pistol aside without knocking
it from her hand. He grabs* MAY *and they fall together
onto the bed. They roll first one direction then the other,
struggling for possession of the gun.*]

SHEPHERD You – shit!!
[*The struggle continues for another moment. A pistol
shot.* SHEPHERD *yelps and rolls away from* MAY. *She gets
quickly to her feet, training the pistol on him as before.
He grips his shoulder, which is bleeding profusely.* MAY,
*panting, sweating, steadies herself, grips the pistol with
both hands, gestures sharply with it.*]

MAY Now, finish – Mister Shepherd! It's too hot – for all this
dancing and dying! Finish!!
[SHEPHERD *stands, constantly gripping, squeezing his
wounded shoulder. He begins re-packing the suitcase,
using only his uninjured arm. He doesn't look at* MAY *now,
but finishes the job as quickly as he can.* MAY *sings, shaky
but clear.*]
'The shelt'ring arm,
So warm,

The proudest gaze,
Ablaze,
The lips that all
Adore:
Did she get what she came for?'
[SHEPHERD *completes packing, closes and snaps the*
suitcase shut. Still training the pistol on him, MAY *quickly*
snatches the suitcase from the opposite side of the bed,
and, never taking her eyes off him, backs slowly out of the
room. SHEPHERD *watches her – squeezes his shoulder –*
flinches – sits on the bed.]
[*Music for scene change: the second act tune, played by*
harmonica, concertina and/or piano.]

Calgary, North West Territories. Autumn, 1891. Morning.
    Atlantic Avenue, dusty, windy. Voices are heard before
anyone is seen.

NETTIE   [*Off.*] Don't push!
SEWARD   [*Off.*] Walk, girl! Walk!!
NETTIE   [*Off.*] What were we doing?!
SEWARD   [*Off.*] Walk!
NETTIE   [*Off.*] What are we doing?!
SEWARD   [*Off.*] Walk!
         [NETTIE *staggers in along the wooden sidewalk. She is*
         pale and thin, her hair around her shoulders, her dress
         soiled.]
NETTIE   We weren't doing a thing! You got no right!
         [SEWARD *follows her in, dragging* LILY *behind him. He*
         wears civilian clothes and hasn't shaved for several days.
         LILY *trembles, her mouth is constantly wet, and she*
         stumbles at every step.]
NETTIE   Where're you taking us?!
SEWARD   Where do you think?
         [*He drags* LILY *forward. She stumbles, collapses, sits at*
         the edge of the filthy sidewalk.]
NETTIE   This isn't even the way to the Police!
SEWARD   [*To* LILY.] You walk, woman, or we'll drag you by your
         heels!

NETTIE	You got no right!
SEWARD	[*Turns on her.*] I've got every right! I've got judgement, haven't I? I see. Everything! I saw everything!
NETTIE	Then how come you never saw where May's gone to?! [SEWARD *grabs her by the throat. She yelps.*]
SEWARD	I knew where she was! All the time! Out there with her Yankee treasure! Her Yankee demon! But she's left him now!
NETTIE	Don't!
SEWARD	He must've run out of money, out of smiles and French silk! 'The woman was arrayed in purple and scarlet colour, and decked with gold!' Where's she gone?!
NETTIE	Don't! [*She pulls away from* SEWARD, *rubs her throat.*] I don't know anything! I never got told anything!
SEWARD	[*Turns to* LILY.] You both know!
NETTIE	May was good, but she never told me anything! She told me, 'Answer the door, Nettie, don't mess yourself, don't scratch,' but that's all!
SEWARD	[*Moves to* LILY, *shouts.*] You know! And Missus Decarmin knows too! [*He stoops, searches* LILY's *face. She shakes her head, closes her eyes and cries.*]
NETTIE	Violet? [*Laughs.*] Who knows what Violet knows?! She don't know anything! I don't even know where she is! Violet went off with some Indian! I heard somebody say she went off for a while with some Indian or half-breed who's a rich man in Montana or somewhere else I never heard of –! [SEWARD *grabs* LILY's *hair. She gasps, but doesn't open her eyes.*]
SEWARD	May Buchanan?!
NETTIE	Lily?! [*She wants to move closer, to protect* LILY, *but she's afraid.*]
SEWARD	[*Pulling* LILY's *head back.*] You know where she's gone! Where is she?!
NETTIE	You got no right!! [ROSS *rushes in, wearing police uniform. He sees* SEWARD *and stops.* NETTIE *sees him and smiles feebly.*]
SEWARD	[*To* LILY.] You, all of you, know! And one of you's going to tell me!!

59

ROSS	Mister Seward!
	[SEWARD *turns, sees him.*]
SEWARD	Get out of here! [*Turns back to* LILY.] Is she trying to get home again?! Is she gone back East?!
ROSS	Mister Seward!
	[SEWARD *releases* LILY, *turns to* ROSS *again.* LILY'*s head slumps forward onto her chest.* NETTIE *scoots past* SEWARD, *goes to* LILY, *sits beside her and holds her.*]
SEWARD	[*At the same time.*] Mister Ross! What are you doing here? Snarling up the investigation? Complicating things!
ROSS	There's no investigation!
SEWARD	Trying to seem important!
ROSS	[*Past* SEWARD, *to the women.*] There's no investigation! Mister Seward's no longer with us!
SEWARD	[*To* ROSS.] Or maybe you've gone over –
ROSS	[*To the women.*] He's no longer with the Police!
SEWARD	– over to their side?!
ROSS	[*As above.*] He's been relieved of his authority!
SEWARD	[*Grabs* ROSS'*s arm.*] I've got all the authority! More than sufficient!
ROSS	[*Pulling free.*] You're drunk, Seward!
SEWARD	And judgement!
ROSS	This is exactly why we had to let you go! You know that!
NETTIE	[*To* LILY, *who hasn't moved.*] It'll be all right, baby!
SEWARD	Passion!
NETTIE	[*As above.*] He's just another old drunk!
SEWARD	'These shall hate the whore, and shall make her desolate and naked!'
ROSS	I think you'd better come with me. Come on! [*He takes* SEWARD'*s arm.*]
SEWARD	'And shall eat her flesh, and burn her with fire!'
ROSS	Quiet down! This is a public thoroughfare.
	[SEWARD *goes along with* ROSS, *but points back toward the women and shouts.*]
SEWARD	These two know! There's probably hundreds that know!
ROSS	Quiet down! You've been warned about this before!
SEWARD	And one of them, one day, has only to tell me!! 'Burn her with fire!'
	[ROSS *leads him out.*]

ROSS	Walk, come on, walk!
	[*They are gone.*]
SEWARD	[*Off.*] 'MYSTERY, BABYLON THE GREAT!'
	[LILY *has stopped crying but has still not moved.* NETTIE *touches* LILY's *chin, then lifts her head gently.*]
NETTIE	You see? It's all just fine now. We're fine. Look at that sky! – Lily...?
	[*No response.* NETTIE *lowers* LILY's *head gently back onto her chest, then scoots even closer to her and holds her tightly.*]
	[*Sings.*] 'A skin so fine,
	Divine,
	A smile that beams
	Bright dreams,
	That thrill me to
	The core:
	But is it what I came for?'
	[*A dog barks, far away. Music for scene change.*]

Vancouver, British Columbia. Winter, 1891-92. Afternoon.

Both rooms of MAY's *two-room house on Water Street, a front room and a bedroom. No door between the two, but because of the angle of the doorway, and because the bedroom is usually much darker, it is difficult to see from one room into the other. Gusty, rainy weather.*

In the bedroom, RAGLAN, *a young waterfront tough, wearing only a woolen cap and drawers, is on the narrow bed, smoking a cigarette.* MAY, *looking drawn and much older, is behind a rickety dressing screen. She pours water, washes herself, rinses her mouth with whiskey.*

In the front room, VIOLET, *also looking much older than before, sits at a small table near a small unsafe-looking cold fireplace. She is mending* MAY's *underclothes. She wears mail order spectacles.*

In the bedroom, MAY *emerges from behind the screen in a cotton shift, drying herself.*

RAGLAN	That's it. Feeling better now?
MAY	I'm all right. You want some fresh water?
	[*She gestures to the screen. He shakes his head 'no.'*]
RAGLAN	Cigarette?
MAY	No.
	[*She gets dressed. A knock at the front door.* VIOLET *looks up.*]
VIOLET	Who's that?
	[*Mister* HANKS, *about the same age as* MAY, *correct and painfully slender, comes into the front room. The following conversations – between* VIOLET *and* HANKS, *between* MAY *and* RAGLAN *– do not overlap but should be carefully synchronized as written.*]
	Oh. Mister Hanks?
HANKS	Good afternoon.
RAGLAN	Somebody else, eh?
VIOLET	We haven't seen you for a while.
HANKS	No.
RAGLAN	Somebody else's out there.
VIOLET	Not for a couple of weeks at least?
HANKS	More like months, I'm afraid.
RAGLAN	More customers – jingle, jingle, jingle!
VIOLET	Haven't been unwell, have you?
HANKS	[*Shakes his head 'no'.*] Just busy, terribly busy.
RAGLAN	Time for me to clear out, eh?
VIOLET	Making heaps of money, Mister Hanks?
MAY	You could stay if you want.
HANKS	My employer makes heaps of money.
MAY	You could talk to Violet.
HANKS	I do well to break even!
RAGLAN	Talk to Violet? [*He laughs.*]
VIOLET	What business did you say you're in?
HANKS	Shipping.
RAGLAN	Where's the treat in talking to Violet?
MAY	Where's the treat in talking to anybody?
	[RAGLAN *grabs her.*]
RAGLAN	You mean there's nicer things to do than talk?
MAY	[*Pulls free.*] I mean, where's the treat in talking. I have to go on out there now.
RAGLAN	Jingle, jingle, jingle!

VIOLET	You want some coffee or anything?
HANKS	No, thank you.
RAGLAN	And I have to make myself 'socially presentable.'
	[*He wiggles his bum at* MAY. *She goes into the front room.*]
VIOLET	[*To* HANKS.] I'm afraid coffee's all I can offer you, way the hell out here!
MAY	There's a swallow or two of Irish, maybe. In my room. Hello, Mister Hanks.
HANKS	How are you, May?
MAY	I'm fine. I'm all right.
	[*In the bedroom,* RAGLAN *gets up, gets dressed in front of a mirror.*]
VIOLET	Mister Hanks was just saying he'd have been back to see you sooner, only he's been terribly busy. Making heaps of money!
HANKS	Scarcely. [*He takes* MAY's *hands in his.*] You don't look all right. You're pale.
MAY	I'm cold. A couple of fingers of Irish –
HANKS	You haven't been sick?
VIOLET	No, she hasn't!
MAY	Maybe a little tired.
	[HANKS *kisses* MAY *near, but not on, the mouth.*]
VIOLET	A money-mad mogul of the shipping trade, that's our Mister Hanks!
MAY	Violet!
	[VIOLET *goes back to her mending.*]
HANKS	I've been thinking about you, May. Nothing but you.
MAY	Doesn't that interfere with your work?
HANKS	[*Holding on to her.*] I look out one of the little windows in my office, and I can see English Bay! Tall ships, taking people to amazing places! To worlds that nobody's ever even written about yet! I look out another little window, and I can see the roof of this house. and I say to myself, 'Poor May. Poor, poor May.'
VIOLET	Poor May.
HANKS	You've been out here six or seven months now. I'll wager you've seen scarcely any of our city.
MAY	I've seen enough.

63

HANKS	And I say to myself, 'I've never even asked poor May out for supper!'
VIOLET	And why the hell not?
MAY	Violet?

[*In the bedroom,* RAGLAN *finishes dressing, admires himself in the mirror.*]

HANKS	So I'm driving you out to Maxie's Hotel for supper. I won't take 'no' for an answer! Maybe we could spend the night.
MAY	I don't think so.
VIOLET	Go ahead! I'll keep an eye on things! It's all I'm fit for!
HANKS	[*To* MAY.] Have you ever been out to Maxie's?
MAY	No.
HANKS	Well, I call that a rotten shame!

[RAGLAN *moves to the doorway between the rooms, looks out.*]

HANKS	Eight months you've graced our great 'Terminal City Of The Far West,' and you've never even been for a bite at Maxie's!
RAGLAN	Maxie's?!

[*He laughs.* HANKS *turns and sees him.* MAY *removes her hands from* HANKS' *grip.*]

Flipping fleabag Maxie's! Flipping trifle-and-cholera-for-dessert Maxie's!

HANKS	You've been there, I'm sure?
RAGLAN	Christ, yes! Maxie's got rats in his kitchen almost as big as I am!

[HANKS *looks him up and down, makes a face.*]

HANKS	Mm. I suppose rats come in all sizes.
RAGLAN	[*Moves toward him.*] What are you trying to say?!
HANKS	You've been in Maxie's kitchen, I'm sure?
RAGLAN	Yeah, they hired me in! To strangle rats!
MAY	Stop it!

[*They both look at her.* VIOLET *titters, without looking up.*]

RAGLAN	Time for me to clear out!
HANKS	The oil in that lamp's created quite a stink in here, May. I guess it's the lamp. [*Glances at* RAGLAN.] Shall we adjourn to the other room?

[*He moves into the bedroom, without waiting for* MAY, *and sits on her bed.* MAY *smiles faintly at* RAGLAN.]

MAY	Bye-bye.
RAGLAN	I'm back here on Wednesday!
MAY	Wednesday.

[*She goes into the bedroom, sits on the bed beside* HANKS. *He takes her hands and sniffs them. As before, conversations in the two rooms are synchronized, not simultaneous.*]

RAGLAN	[*To* VIOLET.] 'Quite a stink in here! I guess it's the lamp!' [*Snorts.*] Flipping Florence Nightingale!! [*He starts out the front door.*]
VIOLET	Raglan!

[*He turns back.*]

HANKS	I'm glad to see you again, May.

[VIOLET *extends her open hand toward* RAGLAN.]

MAY	I'm glad you're glad.
RAGLAN	I already paid.
VIOLET	You're a liar! [*She leaves her hand extended.*]
HANKS	But you're terribly pale!
MAY	I'm sorry.

[RAGLAN *laughs, digs money out of his trousers pocket.*]

HANKS	You should be more careful about the company you keep.
MAY	Maybe.

[RAGLAN *gives money to* VIOLET.]

HANKS	I'd look after you, if you'd let me. Just let me.
VIOLET	*Merci bien. T'es genti'.*
RAGLAN	Pardon me?
VIOLET	French! Never heard anybody speak French before? [*She carefully tucks the money into her bosom.* RAGLAN *watches her. At the same time,* HANKS *begins unbuttoning* MAY's *top.*]
HANKS	I suppose hundreds of men must've offered to look after you.
MAY	I haven't counted them.
RAGLAN	French, eh? I thought you were from California some place.
VIOLET	Who told you that?

[HANKS *has reached* MAY's *waist. She suddenly cries out softly.* RAGLAN *perks up, looks toward the bedroom.* VIOLET *looks too.*]

65

MAY	It's pinned. Let me. [*She finishes unbuttoning, unpinning her clothes.*]
RAGLAN	Old Violet – I guess you must hear some fairly fascinating sounds whispering outa that bedroom, eh?
VIOLET	Time for you to clear out!
HANKS	Lovely.
RAGLAN	Right. Back here on Wednesday! Remind May!
VIOLET	Wednesday.

[*She goes back to her mending.* RAGLAN *goes out, whistling the second act tune. He can be heard for several moments outside the house, whistling, later singing. In the bedroom,* HANKS *helps* MAY *out of her outer clothing, kissing and caressing her at the same time.*]

MAY	You know a lot of things, Mister Hanks. I won't talk, you talk. Tell me more about the tall ships. In English Bay. Where do they go?
HANKS	Wherever you like.
MAY	Wherever I like. To China? Past China?
HANKS	Don't you have any stockings, May? Why don't you put some stockings on?
RAGLAN	[*Unseen, outside, sings.*]

'A skin so fine,
Divine –'

HANKS	[*As* MAY *puts on stockings.*] Lovely.
RAGLAN	[*As above.*]

'A smile that beams
Bright dreams –!'

[*He is heard laughing, then whistling the rest of a verse, which quickly fades.* VIOLET *looks up from her mending, rubs her eyes behind the spectacles.*]

VIOLET	It's late. Isn't it late?

[*But she's talking to nobody in particular. In the bedroom,* HANKS *stands, then kneels at* MAY's *bedside, caresses her stockinged legs.*]

MAY	How much would it cost? To get on board one of those tall ships and just go? And when they reach their destination, you say to them, 'No, not here, farther. Farther on! Don't ever stop till I tell you!'
HANKS	Lovely.

MAY	And maybe, maybe you never have to stop, never have to be still!
HANKS	So lovely.
	[*He embraces* MAY *around the waist. She looks up at the ceiling, then closes her eyes. In the front room,* VIOLET *goes back to her mending, sings.*]
VIOLET	'A blessed sleep,
	So deep –'
MAY	Never.
VIOLET	'Then trumpets call
	Us all –'
MAY	Never.
VIOLET	'To Heaven's gol-
	Den door –'
HANKS	So very lovely.
MAY	Never stop.
VIOLET	'But is it what we came for?'
	[*She laughs to herself.* HANKS *begins making love to* MAY. *After a moment,* SHEPHERD *suddenly walks into the front room, without knocking.* VIOLET *looks up and squints.*]
	Who's that?
	[SHEPHERD *looks at her, doesn't speak. He is haggard, dirty, and has been drinking.* VIOLET *takes off her spectacles, peers, and recognizes him.*]
	Mother of Christ! – She's busy now. She's terribly busy!
	[*She glances toward the bedroom door.* SHEPHERD's *eyes follow hers.*]
SHEPHERD	Tell her to come out here, Violet.
	[*She looks at him, doesn't speak.*]
SHEPHERD	Ask her, please, to come out here!
	[*In the bedroom,* MAY *has opened her eyes. She looks toward the doorway to the front room, listening.* HANKS *continues making love, oblivious. In the front room,* SHEPHERD *looks at* VIOLET *again. She sneers, puts her spectacles back on, and returns to her mending.* SHEPHERD *watches her for an instant, then suddenly grabs the mending from her, removes a long needle from it, and jabs the needle several times deeply into the palm of his hand.*]
VIOLET	Mother of the living Christ!

[SHEPHERD *shows* VIOLET *his bloody palm, as though displaying evidence.*]

SHEPHERD   Goddamn both of you! I've been tracking her for eight months! You think I'm going to stand out here and wait my turn now, like a sailor boy who can't keep his flies buttoned?!!

[*In the bedroom,* MAY *has recognized* SHEPHERD*'s voice, and is trying to disentangle herself from* HANKS.]

HANKS   May? What is it?

SHEPHERD   Call her out here, Violet.

[MAY, *now wearing only her cotton shift and loose stockings, stands and pulls free of* HANKS.]

HANKS   Who is it?

[MAY *puts a finger to her lips, gestures for him to be patient a moment. She turns and moves to the doorway.*]

SHEPHERD   [*Sees her.*] May.

MAY   Mister Shepherd.

VIOLET   I told him you're busy!

[MAY *looks at* SHEPHERD*'s stabbed hand which he still holds extended.*]

MAY   You're bleeding. As usual.

[*With his sound hand,* SHEPHERD *takes money from his pocket.*]

VIOLET   Who in hell does he think he is, coming in here, taking liberties?!

[SHEPHERD *wipes the money through the blood in his other palm several times. In the bedroom,* HANKS *adjusts his clothing, then stands, peering out into the front room.*]

VIOLET   Whatever happened to that lovely old thing called courtesy?!

[SHEPHERD *extends the blood-soaked money toward* MAY. *She watches him, but doesn't move.*]

He's blind and vicious drunk!!

[*Without rising from her chair,* VIOLET *suddenly reaches out and snatches the money from* SHEPHERD, *and tucks it into her bosom. At the same time,* HANKS *moves up quite close behind* MAY, *who is still in the doorway.*]

HANKS   What is it? Come back, May, we'll talk about tall ships and distant places – May ...?

[MAY *turns in the doorway and stares at* HANKS *for a moment. Then she turns again and moves swiftly to* SHEPHERD. *She takes his injured hands in hers, and studies his wound.* VIOLET *and* HANKS *watch, frozen.* MAY *looks up into* SHEPHERD's *eyes, then says, over her shoulder, without really looking around.*]

MAY   I'm finished, Mister Hanks. Sorry. I'm finished for the day.

[SHEPHERD *reaches out for her and she moves forward, allows herself to be held by him. Music for scene change.*]

Both rooms of MAY's *Vancouver house. Evening of the same day. Sounds of a persistent slow, heavy rain; occasional splashing carriages or horses on the street outside.*

    The bedroom is dark, unoccupied.

    MAY *and* SHEPHERD *are sitting on the floor in the front room. A fire in the small fireplace has burnt down to embers, and they have roasted potatoes in it. They sit near the fireplace now, and finish eating the charred potato skins.* MAY *is dressed, except for shoes and stockings.* SHEPHERD *is barefoot, wears his trousers and an unbuttoned shirt. His hand is bandaged with a strip of greyish material from a petticoat or curtain.*

SHEPHERD   May? ... I love you.

    [*He leans close to kiss her. She turns her head aside. He kisses her neck.*]

    I do love you.

MAY   So. You showed me, didn't you?

SHEPHERD   I wanted to. It wasn't all love though. Some of it was anger.

MAY   Some of it always is. Maybe most of it.

SHEPHERD   Christ! I didn't know what was happening to me! Not for eight months! I asked everybody, but nobody knew! Violet disappeared, Lily disappeared! Nettie told me you'd gone home, back East. I knew you, I knew which direction you'd pick – but how far? Here or in the States? What would you be calling yourself, who would

	you be with? Then somebody from the Police told me you'd been –
MAY	You went to the Police?!
SHEPHERD	I told you, I was crazy!
MAY	Christ knows! [*She finishes eating.*]
SHEPHERD	They told me you'd been seen in Portland.
	[MAY *laughs.*]
	So I sold everything at Sheep River, went to Portland! I stopped in every little goddamned tiny place along the way – any place with more than two men and three horses – and I gave out your description! I sung your praises in every saloon and hotel lobby, and waited for somebody to pick up the scent!
MAY	Well. I'm famous.
SHEPHERD	I haven't got a penny – or a friend – or any patience left. But nothing's changed otherwise. I love you. I want you. [*He tries to kiss her again. She stands and moves away.*]
MAY	Nothing's changed with me either, Shepherd.
	[VIOLET *suddenly comes in from outside, dripping wet, a threadbare shawl or cloak around her shoulders.*]
VIOLET	Mother of Christ! Is this where poor old Noah lives?! Tell him to get started on that bloody ark!! [*She closes the front door and shakes herself.*] You wouldn't believe how hard it is to locate a pint of hootch in this Godforsaken town! Two thirds of those bastards out there actually drink *tea*! And think we're going to drink it with them! [*She reaches inside the shawl or cloak and takes out a bottle of whiskey.*] Didn't cost me a penny though! Well – you don't want to hear about that! [*She takes the cork out of the bottle, takes a long swig from it. Gasps.*] Mother of Christ! [*Sniffs the bottle.*] Shooo! Guaranteed to cure glanders, anthrax and shipping fever! [*She laughs and hands the bottle to* MAY, *who takes a long drink.*] I smell potatoes?
SHEPHERD	We just ate the last of them.
VIOLET	Oh, thanks very much!
	[MAY *hands the whiskey bottle to* SHEPHERD. *He drinks.*] I don't like to eat anymore anyways. It only keeps me alive!

[*She removes her shawl or cloak, and hangs it on the back of a chair near the fireplace. At the same time,* SHEPHERD *pours a bit of the booze into the palm of his bandaged hand.*]

MAY   [*Watching him.*] Doesn't that burn?

SHEPHERD   Naw. Not much. [*Suddenly the liquor reaches his wound. He gasps, slams the bottle down, gets to his feet, howls.*] Oooooww! Oh shit!!

           [*He dances around the room.* MAY *and* VIOLET *laugh.*]

SHEPHERD   Oh holy mother of shit!! [*He waves his hands through the air.*]

VIOLET   [*Grins, maternal.*] That's good! That means it's working!

SHEPHERD   Shit! [*Gradually he stops dancing and waving his hand.*]

VIOLET   We really ought to put a fresh wrapping on that!

           [SHEPHERD *retreats from her.*]

MAY   I'll manage him, Violet. You go on to bed.

           [SHEPHERD *retrieves the whiskey, takes a big gulp.*]

VIOLET   Where's the treat in going to bed? I never sleep anymore! Never do anything else either!

MAY   [*Kisses her.*] You can rest at least.

VIOLET   I never rest anymore. I just remember. I can't stand myself! [*She starts toward the bedroom, then turns back.*] You didn't have no other visitors while I was out?

MAY   No.

VIOLET   None of your regulars? [*She glances at* SHEPHERD.]

MAY   Violet! No man, no matter how regular, is going out in that flood, wading all the way down to the end of Water Street, just to leave his calling card with you or me! [SHEPHERD *comes up behind her, puts his arm around her.* MAY *doesn't resist.*]

VIOLET   [*In the bedroom doorway.*] You wouldn't think so, would you? Hell, I don't get many calling cards anymore, rain or shine. Don't even want them! But tonight – I'm out there, dodging puddles, looking and smelling like a drowned rat – and this big guy starts after me!

MAY   [*Smiles.*] This big guy?

VIOLET   Luck of the Irish, eh? And I'm not even Irish, thank Christ! But here he comes, stumbling along after me, drunk I guess, wheezing like an old horse! Not saying a word! I don't mind telling you, I was scared! He stuck to

	me! I stepped up my pace, came down alleys instead of streets, went right past here and doubled back again a couple of times – finally lost him!
MAY	Well, he doesn't sound like much of a loss!
SHEPHERD	[*Still holding* MAY, *drinks more whiskey.*] I wonder what he wanted though – following Violet like that!
VIOLET	[*Offended.*] What do you mean? What do you think he wanted?! What do you mean?
MAY	Go to bed, Violet.
SHEPHERD	I don't mean anything! I mean, you said yourself you look like a drowned rat, and smell –!
VIOLET	[*Coming back into the front room.*] So what?! It was pitch black out there, and I still got my shape, don't I?! I still got my walk! You don't believe some man, some big guy in an expensive fur coat, could mistake me in that Christ-awful downpour for a lady of twenty-five, twenty-eight?! I still got my waistline, you know, I still got my –!
MAY	Violet! Go to bed.
	[VIOLET *looks at her, then nods, and goes into the bedroom, where she lights a small smoky lamp, then removes her wet shoes and stockings. In the front room,* MAY *unwraps* SHEPHERD*'s arm from around her, and leads him to sit at the table, where she unwraps and inspects his injured hand.*]
	Let's have a look. – Doesn't it burn?
SHEPHERD	Mm. Like hellfire!
	[*They laugh.* MAY *takes a strip of fabric from* VIOLET*'s sewing box, and rewraps the hand. At the same time,* SHEPHERD *drinks more, then starts to embrace her.*]
MAY	Careful! I don't want to aggravate your injury.
SHEPHERD	You ought to help me forget it!
	[*He sets the bottle down and kisses her. She turns her head, as before.*]
MAY	You ought to get some sleep.
SHEPHERD	I'm not tired!
MAY	Liar. You look like what the five-month widow found – when she dug up her husband, to get his gold teeth!
SHEPHERD	Violet's got the bed. Where do we sleep?
MAY	Where do *you* sleep? Well, there's an extra blanket, and

	there's the floor. Or there's a hotel every couple of blocks all the way down to the harbour.
SHEPHERD	I'll go to a hotel. And you'll come with me.
MAY	You said you don't have a penny.
SHEPHERD	I got enough for a hotel! And tomorrow you're coming away from all this, saying goodbye to this pisshole Vancouver! Coming away for good, with me!
MAY	I'm not, you know. [*She stands, starts to move away. He grabs her.*]
SHEPHERD	I mean, for good!
MAY	I know what you mean! I know what I mean. [*She pulls free and starts toward the bedroom.* SHEPHERD *leaps to his feet and grabs her again, holds her. In the bedroom,* VIOLET *sits very still on the bed, listening.*]
SHEPHERD	May! Nothing's changed! Not a thing! You traveled on, like you thought you had to! But I traveled on too! I found you! We can go on traveling, if that's what you want! But together! I love you! Nothing has changed! [*She frees herself again.*]
MAY	Goddamn you! You're too bloody right, nothing's changed! What did I ever ask for from anybody but change, a little change?! [*He starts for her again. She hits him.*] Goddamn you, Shepherd, hands off! [*He doesn't touch her, but blocks her path to the bedroom.* VIOLET *stands, watching, listening.*] Listen very carefully. Make up your mind. Some woman, some day, may take what you've got to offer. To lie down wrapped up in your rules and your laws! To let you be her judge, her reason to breathe, or not to! Her food and her fire – but make up your mind, here and now, Thomas Shepherd, that woman is not, not ever, going to be me!
SHEPHERD	I love you.
MAY	Oh, who doesn't?! Christ knows! I wouldn't trade a half-pound of dog shit for all the stuff you call love! What I mean to have is way – way beyond that! [*She tries to push past him, into the bedroom. He holds her.*]

SHEPHERD	Jesus! *You* listen! I broke myself – listen! – I went broke finding you!!
MAY	[*Suddenly stops pushing, leans against him; quietly.*] They've got ships, you know, tall ships. Out in English Bay. Departures every day. You get in a little boat and paddle out there to them! And they welcome you aboard and don't even ask your destination, because they're all headed the same way, west, to China and way beyond, the Spice Islands, and way way beyond!
SHEPHERD	May – [*He kisses her.*]
MAY	[*Looking him in the eye.*] How much do figure it costs? To just go on? Never to say, 'Here's where I stop'? How much would that cost? Oh God, please, not much – please – not more than I've got! [*She suddenly pushes again and knocks him aside. She goes into the bedroom, to the far side of the bed, and lies down.* SHEPHERD *starts to follow, but* VIOLET *steps into his path. Nearby, outside the house, a dog barks intermittently.*]
SHEPHERD	May!
VIOLET	Time for you to clear out!
SHEPHERD	[*Past* VIOLET; *to* MAY.] I'm not leaving here alone!!
MAY	[*Closes her eyes.*] No more words!
SHEPHERD	May, you can keep a house if you have to! I'll buy you a new big house somewhere! You can have all the ladies you like! Jesus Christ, you can have other men if you have to! I'll get some more money!!
MAY	No more.
SHEPHERD	But I'm not leaving here alone tonight!!
VIOLET	[*Bracing herself in the doorway.*] Mister Shepherd, we got a gun here! Don't make me get the gun!
SHEPHERD	I know everything you are or could be, May!
MAY	No more.
SHEPHERD	And goddamnit, I worship you!! [*Blocked by* VIOLET, *he whirls away from the doorway, goes to the table and drinks more whiskey.*]
VIOLET	[*At the same time.*] 'I worship you!' [*Laughs.*] You're no different from any of the others! They come to worship, or beat her up, or spit on her! Mother of Christ, they love us and they hate us, they love us and they hate us, May!

74

SHEPHERD	You're drunk, Violet!
VIOLET	On what?! Your cowshit poetry?! You're the one drinking all our booze, taking all our time, and not paying one red cent for –!!
	[*Someone prowling outside the front door of the house stumbles over a bench or clatters into a rainpipe.*]
VIOLET	[*Hisses.*] Listen! What's that?!
	[SHEPHERD *turns toward the front door. In the bedroom,* MAY *opens her eyes.*]
VIOLET	Mother of Christ, I'll bet it's him!
SHEPHERD	Who?!
VIOLET	Sssh. My friend – followed me on the street – my big rich guy! Listen.
	[SHEPHERD *moves slowly, silently to the front door.*]
MAY	[*From the bed.*] Violet –?
	[VIOLET *turns to her.*]
VIOLET	Sssh, baby! You rest, just rest easy.
	[MAY *doesn't move, but keeps her eyes open. In the front room,* SHEPHERD *suddenly throws the front door open, and pulls a large wet man in a buffalo coat into the room. It is* SEWARD. *He is dressed in filthy sodden civilian clothes, looks ancient.*]
VIOLET	[*Watching.*] What is that?!
	[SEWARD *yelps as* SHEPHERD *twists his arm, and slams him down in a chair near the small table.* VIOLET *moves nearer and they recognize* SEWARD.]
VIOLET	Mother of God!
SHEPHERD	Shit!
VIOLET	'Walk, Constable, walk!'
SHEPHERD	[*Shoving him.*] What do you want here?!
	[*In the bedroom,* MAY *props herself up on one elbow. stares out into the front room.*]
VIOLET	It was you – out in that flood – *you* came after me!
	[SHEPHERD *seizes* SEWARD *by the neck.*]
SHEPHERD	I said, what do you want?!
VIOLET	[*Backs away.*] Careful! Has he got a gun?!
	[SHEPHERD *searches* SEWARD *briefly.*]
SEWARD	[*Trembling.*] No, I – I – No, I'm not – I'm unarmed!
VIOLET	You're unhinged!!
SEWARD	Oh, you had a – a fire. It's nice and – warm!

SHEPHERD	You've got no goddamn business here! You've got no right!
SEWARD	Have so! Have every right! Not just Police right anymore! I left the Police! They've got no judgement, no passion! I'm way beyond that! [*Shrugs off the buffalo coat, still trembling; looks around.*] Darling May's come down in the world, eh?
SHEPHERD	Put that back on, you skinless shit! You're not staying!! [*He tries to pull the buffalo coat back over* SEWARD*'s shoulders.*]
VIOLET	You smell like the great buffalo burial ground!!
MAY	[*Calls softly from the bedroom.*] Violet ...? [VIOLET *hurries into the bedroom, sits beside* MAY *and takes her hand.*]
SEWARD	[*At the same time.*] Yes! She's in there!! [*He stands, stares toward the bedroom.* SHEPHERD *moves between him and the doorway.* SEWARD *stares past or through* SHEPHERD.]
SHEPHERD	I ought to kill you, here and now! I ought to finish what I started back there!
SEWARD	I see you, May Buchanan!
VIOLET	[*To* MAY.] He don't see nothing, angel!
SEWARD	'They shall make her desolate and naked –'
SHEPHERD	[*Threatening to hit him.*] Get the hell out of here!
SEWARD	'– and shall eat her flesh, and burn her with fire!'
MAY	[*To no one.*] No more words.
SEWARD	'Alleluja! And her smoke rose up for ever and ever!'
SHEPHERD	[*Grabs him, shoves him toward the door.*] You crazy shit!
VIOLET	[*Caresses* MAY.] Baby, baby ...
SEWARD	[*Trying to shake* SHEPHERD *off.*] Wait, wait, wait! [*He takes money from his pockets, handfuls of it, and throws it down on the table.*] There, there! Isn't that enough?!
SHEPHERD	Enough for what?!
SEWARD	Her! I came for her! I mean to have her!
SHEPHERD	You're not having anybody, you piece of filth! [*He grabs* SEWARD *again, but* SEWARD *will not be budged; he resists* SHEPHERD *like a dead weight.*] Look! She's finished, she can't be bought, she's finished with all that!
SEWARD	She can't be finished! Not yet! Oh, I watched them

	coming in and out of her door for two Christly days now! Who told you she's finished?!
SHEPHERD	I'm telling you, she is! I told her she is!
SEWARD	You told her?! Who gave you that right?!
SHEPHERD	Who gave me –?!
VIOLET	[*At the same time, to* MAY.] Blind and vicious drunk, both of them!
SHEPHERD	[*At the same time, to* SEWARD.] I did!!
VIOLET	Who gave either of them any rights?!
SHEPHERD	I gave myself the right!! I found her, I won her back! I'm taking her away, giving her some kind of life, whatever she wants!!
	[*In spite of* SHEPHERD's *resistance,* SEWARD *staggers forward, toward the bedroom, taking* SHEPHERD *with him.*]
SEWARD	May Buchanan!!
SHEPHERD	God Almighty!
SEWARD	I see you, May Buchanan! I see my darling May!!
VIOLET	[*Shouts at* SHEPHERD.] Get that sick son of a bitch away from here!!
SHEPHERD	Move!!
	[*He punches* SEWARD *in the gut.* SEWARD *falls to his knees.* SHEPHERD *moves around him, tries to drag him away, but* SEWARD *still will not budge. He shouts toward the nearby bedroom doorway.*]
SEWARD	Here I am, to burn you, May! Please! To purify and redeem! To save you from the judgement that fell on Lily Reeves!!
VIOLET	Lily?!
	[MAY *starts up from the bed.* VIOLET *holds her back.*]
SEWARD	She's dead! Didn't know that, did you?!
HEPHERD	You're lying!
SEWARD	Lily Reeves is dead and rotted!!
MAY	[*Not moving.*] Lily.
SEWARD	Bloated and burst like a poisoned dog! Coroner refused to touch her remains!!
VIOLET	Shut him up, Shepherd!!
	[SHEPHERD *grabs* SEWARD *again by both shoulders.*]
SEWARD	We sank her in quicklime!! And your sweet little Nettie!!
HEPHERD	Get up, goddamn you! Walk!!

[*In spite of him,* SEWARD *crawls nearer the bedroom doorway.*]

SEWARD   Nettie McDowell! She's in prison! Nine years, hard labour!!

[*Exhausted and in pain from his wounded hand,* SHEPHERD *retreats momentarily.*]

SHEPHERD   Oh, oh, Jesus!

[*He reels to the table, finishes the bottle of whiskey.* SEWARD *crawls forward another few feet, but stops at the bedroom threshold, shouts across it.*]

SEWARD   Nine years! I saw to that! I persisted! I spoke out, where others were silent!

MAY   Nettie.

SEWARD   But who made her into what she was, darling May?! Who taught her to sweat in the sty?!!

MAY   Little Nettie.

VIOLET   Shepherd?!!

[SHEPHERD, *now drunk and dazed, turns back toward* SEWARD, *but only stares, doesn't move toward him.*]

SEWARD   Who?! Who taught them all, all the hundreds, all of them, the filthiness of fornication?!!

MAY   No more.

[*She pushes* VIOLET *away and lies back again. closes her eyes.*]

SEWARD   Who handed each of them the golden cup of abomination?!!

[VIOLET *growls, stands suddenly, and charges into the front room.*]

VIOLET   That's it!

[*She seizes* SEWARD *by one arm.* SHEPHERD *looks on, in a queasy stupor.*]

You're the one who's got to smoke and burn, Mister!!

SEWARD   Who taught them – tainted them?!!

[VIOLET *propels him toward the smoldering fireplace.*]

VIOLET   You're the one who's got to be burnt alive!!

SEWARD   May! Buchanan!!

[VIOLET *falls on him with her full weight. He half-crumples.* VIOLET *thrusts his hand into the fireplace embers, as* SHEPHERD *watches.* SEWARD *screams. In the bedroom,* MAY *does not move.*]

MAY   No more.
[*Gasping, whimpering,* SEWARD *shoves* VIOLET *off, and crawls away from the fireplace.*]

SEWARD   May – Buchanan –!
[SHEPHERD *kicks or shoves him with his foot.*]

SHEPHERD   Get out of here now!
[VIOLET *gets to her feet, staggers toward the bedroom doorway.*]

VIOLET   Pathetic scum-loving bastard!
[*She stops in the doorway. She and* SHEPHERD *watch* SEWARD *as he gets slowly, painfully to his feet, trembling more than ever. In the bedroom,* MAY *remains motionless.*]

SEWARD   'Babylon the great is fallen, is fallen' – May Buchanan! – 'and is become the habitation of devils' – May Buchanan! – 'and the hold of every foul spirit' – May Buchanan! [*Holding and squeezing his already livid burnt hand, he shambles toward the front door.*] I'm only here for her! Here to save her!

VIOLET   [*Softly.*] Drunken, slime-eating, shit-breathing poor bastard!

SEWARD   '– and a cage of every unclean and hateful bird!' [*He staggers out, disappears, but can be heard outside, clattering along, falling over things, screaming.*] May Buchanan! 'Come out of her!' I say: 'Come out of her!'

VIOLET   Soulless sightless bastard! [*She moves quickly to the front door, stares out, making sure* SEWARD *doesn't come back.*]

SEWARD   [*Farther off.*] May!! Buchanan!!!

VIOLET   [*Shouts into the darkness.*] Don't make us get the law after you!

SEWARD   [*Still farther.*] May –!!

VIOLET   Jelly-brain bastard.
[*She remains, staring out, watching.* SHEPHERD *tries to drink more from the empty whiskey bottle, then realizes it's empty. He throws it into the fireplace, and weaves toward the bedroom doorway.*]

SEWARD   [*Very far away. almost inaudible.*] May ...!!
[SHEPHERD *looks into the bedroom, at* MAY, *who has not moved.*]

SHEPHERD	Are you – all right?
	[*No response. He moves into the bedroom, to the bed.* VIOLET *turns from the front door, and sees him enter the bedroom. She thinks about this for a moment, then moves to the table, and quickly gathers up* SEWARD'*s money. She shoves it into her bosom, then grabs her shawl or cloak, wraps it around herself, and steps outside the front door. At the same time,* SHEPHERD *lies down on the bed beside* MAY, *without touching her.*]
SHEPHERD	I said, are you all right?
MAY	How do you think I am? How should I be?
	[*He scoots nearer, touching her only lightly.* VIOLET *may occasionally be glimpsed, patrolling outside the open front door, until otherwise noted.*]
SHEPHERD	All I ever wanted – the one thing I ever really wanted in my life – is to take you away from filth like that! Do you know?
	[*No response. He scoots still closer, starts to kiss her. She sits up abruptly, puts her hands over her face.* SHEPHERD *scoots nearer again, caresses her back and buttocks.*]
	Why don't you let me? Jesus, you heard what he said! You want to finish like that? Like Lily, like Nettie?!
	[*She stands, turns on him violently.*]
MAY	No more! Don't speak their names!! You're no better than him! Seward! You've just got a different set of rules and laws you think can save us! You've just got a different fire to burn us in! You're no better!
SHEPHERD	[*Sits up on the bed.*] Don't talk that way!
MAY	Don't talk at all! Where's the treat?! Words! Nettie McDowell had a few words, like bubbles on her lip, sweet! Words can't free her now! Goddamn them, damn you all!
	[SHEPHERD *stands, starts toward her. She retreats to the other side of the bed.*]
	Lily Reeves! Had words and songs too – enough to howl, to cry for help! But she's dead, helpless, rotten, and quicklime ate her cry!! Violet Decarmin, swiping at men and demons with a tongue like a razor! But I could tell

her, men and demons always come back! They search you out and pin you down! No more!!

[*He follows her around the bed.*]

HEPHERD   Please, May –!

[*He reaches for her. She holds him off with both hands, strong.*]

MAY   Thomas Shepherd! Oh, he spreads a whole blanket of words! 'Lie down here, May! It's safe here, it's warm and soft and final beside me!' But not *free*, Mister Shepherd. Freedom's not had with words! I've no more time to invest in you, in any of you, any of it! I am – *traveling*!! No more. I have said my last word.

[*She sits on the bed and stares at him, stonily. His face hardens.*]

HEPHERD   Right then!

[*He grabs her by both shoulders. She does not resist.*]

Missus Buchanan!!

[*He pushed her back on the bed and lies on top of her.*]

I'll make this flesh hear me then! I'll make the inside listen – since the outside wants to be deaf!!

[*He kisses her as hard as he can on the mouth. She wiggles one leg free and knees him in the crotch. He contracts. She writhes out from under him, and scrambles off the far side of the bed. She starts around the end of the bed, toward the doorway into the front room. Groaning into an upright position, SHEPHERD reaches for her. She dodges, but he catches her by her skirt, and pulls her back. She whirls on him and reaches for his eyes, but SHEPHERD twines one hand roughly through her hair, pulls her head back and kisses her, pulling her body against his tightly with his other arm. He kisses her hard and long, then leans back slightly, still holding her by her hair. He waits for her to respond.*]

MAY   [*Between her teeth.*] You bloody goddamn –!

[*SHEPHERD frees his hand from around her waist, and slaps her suddenly, quite hard.*]

EPHERD   No words, Missus Buchanan!

[*He throws her down on the bed. MAY gasps, recovers from the slap.*]

MAY   You goddamn –!

[*He slaps her again, harder. She falls back on the bed from the force of the blow.*]

SHEPHERD No words! You're the one who said 'No words'!!

MAY ... Shepherd —

[*Another slap, only slightly less forceful. She sobs involuntarily, and* SHEPHERD *falls onto her again.*]

SHEPHERD No words!! You said!!

[*As he starts to kiss her neck and breasts,* MAY *wriggles a bit, moaning, and reaches under her pillow. But* SHEPHERD *looks up, sees what she's after, and reaches for the pistol too. The pistol appears, and they struggle over it, as they did once before. Finally* SHEPHERD *wrests the gun from* MAY, *and leaps off the bed. He aims the pistol directly at her. She slowly sits up, staring him in the eye. She starts to stand.*]

No, May!

[*He steps nearer, presses the pistol mouth into her chest, between her breasts, and cocks the hammer.*]

No.

[MAY *is still. She looks up at him, and opens her mouth as if to speak.*]

No!

[*He swiftly moves the pistol from her chest to her lips, and rests the barrel lightly between them.*]

You said, 'No more words. No talk.' But I'm going to tell you, May! I'm going to tell you – inside – where you can't stop yourself listening!

[*Pressing the pistol against her teeth, not too hard, he forces her to lie back on the bed again.*]

You'll listen. Inside! To every thing I have to say ... There, you'll understand ... You'll talk back too.

[MAY *is lying back full-length.* SHEPHERD *straddles her, sits on her and very rapidly shifts the pistol aim from her mouth to the side of her neck. He bends forward and kisses her.* VIOLET *might or might not be seen, outside the front door of the house, but she is heard singing at this point, slowly, gently.*]

VIOLET 'A skin so fine,
Divine –'

[SHEPHERD *sits up, looks down at* MAY. *She stares back at* him, impassive. He bends forward again. She turns her head aside. He lies down on top of her, shifting the cocked pistol to her side, just beneath her arm.]

VIOLET 'A smile that beams
Bright dreams –'

SHEPHERD Please – Now – [*He kisses her neck and breasts.*]

VIOLET 'That thrill me to
The core –'

SHEPHERD Now. Talk to me, May. [*He kisses her more and more angrily, passionately.*]

VIOLET 'But is it what I came for?!'
[*She chuckles, then hums, probably unseen now. In the bedroom,* SHEPHERD *keeps the pistol shoved into* MAY's *side, while kissing her, making love to her, speaking between kisses that are more like bites.*]

SHEPHERD Talk. Not with words. Not with your mouth. Tell me – I don't leave here alone – Tell me – Now – You – Yourself – Tell me –!
[*Using one hand, he has half-undressed her by now. He kisses her breasts, then her mouth again, harder than ever.*]

SHEPHERD Tell me!!
[*He stares at her. Suddenly* MAY *spits deliberately, vehemently, right into his face.*]

SHEPHERD God forgive you –
[*The pistol is fired, a very loud report.* MAY *shudders, coughs softly, and lies still.* SHEPHERD *is on top of her.* VIOLET *runs into the front room.*]

VIOLET May?! [*She hurls herself into the bedroom, and sees the two bodies on the bed.*]

VIOLET Mother of Christ! What is it?!
[*She grabs* SHEPHERD, *tears at him.*]
You – you killed her! [*She drags him off* MAY, *and sees all the blood.*] You murdered her!!
[SHEPHERD *stands and staggers backward, looking at his hands, dazed. He has left the pistol on the bed, near* MAY. VIOLET *sits or lies beside* MAY *on the bed, and tries to lift her.*]
Baby, look at me!

83

[MAY *doesn't move or make a sound.* VIOLET *turns to* SHEPHERD.]

You killed her!!

SHEPHERD   [*Hoarse, stunned.*] Yes.

[VIOLET *lays* MAY *gently back on the bed.*]

VIOLET   Mother of Christ! [*She stands, blood-smeared.*]

SHEPHERD   [*Staggering.*] Yes! Inside!

[VIOLET *turns back to* MAY, *one last attempt.*]

VIOLET   May! Angel?! [*She touches* MAY'*s neck, feels for a pulse.*]

SHEPHERD   [*Something like a laugh.*] She heard though! I know she heard me –!

VIOLET   [*Turns on him.*] Bloody-minded bastard! I'm going for help!

[*She starts out of the bedroom.* SHEPHERD *grabs her, stares at her without seeing her.*]

SHEPHERD   She understood! I know she did! She's – free now!

[*He releases* VIOLET *and stumbles back to the bed. He sits beside* MAY, *lifts her, cradles her in his arms.* VIOLET *watches, frozen.*]

SHEPHERD   She's free. She's – there now – and free –!

[*He kisses her again, hard.* MAY *shudders, almost imperceptibly, then suddenly reaches down, seizes the pistol from among the bloody bedclothes, lifts it, aims it directly into* SHEPHERD'*s side and fires it twice.* VIOLET *starts to scream, but chokes it.* SHEPHERD *is dead without a cry. His body slumps and falls across* MAY.]

VIOLET   May!! [*She rushes to the bed.*] Baby?!! [*She drags* SHEPHERD'*s body off* MAY, *and rolls it to one side, near the edge of the bed.*] Mother of suffering God –! [*She sits and holds* MAY, *who has not opened her eyes since she was shot.*]

MAY   [*A whisper.*] No more –

VIOLET   What, baby?! I'm getting you a doctor! I'll find one!!

[*She starts to stand.* MAY *clings to her violently.*]

MAY   No!! No more –

[VIOLET *sits again, takes the pistol from* MAY'*s hand and tucks it into her own belt.*]

VIOLET   But, oh God, you're bleeding – you're bleeding, baby!!

[*Without opening her eyes,* MAY *scoots to the edge of the bed and tries to stand.* VIOLET *helps her somehow to a* more or less erect position, standing beside her, holding her.]

Please, let me get us a doctor!!

MAY [*A coarse wet whisper.*] No! No, the –!

VIOLET What?

[MAY *stumbles forward toward the bedroom doorway, her eyes still closed.* VIOLET *supports and guides her, wrapped around her.*]

MAY Harbour. Bay. Tall ships. A little boat!! English. Bay!!

VIOLET All right then! Come on, baby! Angel!

[*They have entered and half-crossed the front room, wound together. As they pass a chair,* VIOLET *seizes the buffalo coat which* SEWARD *left behind, and quickly, awkwardly wraps it around both of them.*]

Yes – all right – both of us – out of this – I got all the money – all we need – for sure – for good –!

[*They stagger out the open front door.* MAY *has not once opened her eyes.*]

'Walk, woman! Walk!!'

[*They are gone.*]

[*In the bedroom,* SHEPHERD's *body suddenly slides from the bed, onto the floor, smeared with light from the smoky kerosene lamp.*]

[*There is a tentative knock outside the open front door, and Mister* HANKS *appears, dressed more or less for a formal dinner. He looks around the disordered front room.*]

HANKS May? Hello? [*He notices the light in the bedroom, and creeps toward it very slowly.*] It's me. I'm back, May. I told you I'd come back. [*He arrives at the bedroom doorway, is very tentative about looking in.*] I told you I had something planned for us. Something special. May...? [*He looks into the bedroom, and sees no one at first. He tiptoes into the room a few steps.*] May...?

[*He looks down and sees* SHEPHERD's *body. He stiffens, inhales sharply, then turns and starts toward the front door, as fast as he can. Just as he reaches the front door,* SEWARD *appears in the doorway, blocking his path.*]

SEWARD May Buchanan?!!

[*Music for scene change.*]

English Bay, near Vancouver, British Columbia. The same night.

The beach: rocks, sand and trees. A very old rowboat, the prow of which bobs in the water.

Before anyone is seen, a dog is heard barking, quite loud, nearby. After a moment, its bark fades into the sounds of a calm sea and a gentle wind through the treetops. It has stopped raining. Moonlight.

VIOLET comes in, dragging MAY along. MAY is deathly weak and pale. They are both barefoot, wrapped together in SEWARD's buffalo coat.

MAY   Harbour –

VIOLET   Yes. We're here, baby! We're here. Please – can't you –?

MAY   English Bay!

VIOLET   [*As she spots it.*] A little boat!

MAY   Yes.

VIOLET   It's here, Mother of Christ! Oh, we're all here!
[*They struggle toward the rowboat together. MAY's eyes remain closed to the very end.*]
Come on – a few more steps – you can –
[*Sings, resolutely.*] 'A blessed sleep,
So deep,
Then trumpets call
Us all –'
[*They reach the rowboat, and VIOLET starts to help MAY into it.*]

MAY   Har – bour –

VIOLET   [*Encouraging her, sings.*]
'To Heaven's gol-
Den door:
But is it –?'
[*SEWARD suddenly charges out onto the far end of the beach. His filthy clothes are now even more drenched. He roars.*]

SEWARD   May!! Buchanan!!

VIOLET   Mother of Christ!!
[*She loses her hold on MAY, who slips from beneath the*

buffalo coat, and onto the sand near the rowboat, half-leaning against it.]

SEWARD   [*Moves down the beach toward them.*] I see you! I always see you!!

VIOLET   Raving bastard!
[*She drops the buffalo coat near* MAY, *and turns to* SEWARD.]

SEWARD   May Buchanan! I have you now!

VIOLET   You have nothing! She's going free!! Stop!!
[*As* SEWARD *continues toward them,* VIOLET *whips* MAY's *pistol out of her belt, and aims it at* SEWARD. *He stops.*]

VIOLET   Don't think I won't!! I'll open a gateway through your guts the Mayor and his Sunday carriage could drive through!!

SEWARD   [*Smiles.*] Is that the murder weapon?
[*He reaches for the pistol.* VIOLET *backs up a step or two, and cocks the hammer.*]

VIOLET   Damn your soul, Seward!

SEWARD   No!!
[*During the following exchange,* MAY *somehow manages, gasping and shaking, to crawl over the side of the old rowboat, and to lie down, invisible, within it.*]

SEWARD   My soul is purified! Don't you see it shining?! It has wrestled and cast down its passion! But she – she –!
[*He tries to move past* VIOLET, *toward* MAY. VIOLET *intercepts and holds him off with the gun.*]
Missus May Buchanan, I arrest you for the wilful and premeditated murder of one Thomas Shepherd!

VIOLET   You're not police anymore!!

SEWARD   And for spreading the stench of your gold and scarlet flesh through the lives of – of hundreds! Hundreds!!
'MYSTERY! BABYLON THE GREAT! MOTHER OF HARLOTS!!'

VIOLET   Now I'm going to kill you!!!
[*She starts to squeeze the pistol trigger. Before she can,* SEWARD *reaches out suddenly, seizes the gun, and strikes* VIOLET *across the face with the pistol butt. She falls without a sound, and does not move again.* SEWARD *grins, steps over* VIOLET's *body, staggers up to the rowboat, and aims the pistol into it.*]

SEWARD   All right, crawl out of there!
[*No response.* MAY *is unseen, inside the boat.*]
Now! No more escape for you, my lady! I have you!!
[*No response.* SEWARD *lowers the hammer of the pistol,
tucks it into his belt, and crawls into the rowboat.*] Look
at me! I won't be laughed at!
[*He grabs* MAY *by her arms, and tries to pull her up. She
can be seen now, motionless, silent, in* SEWARD's
trembling grip.] [*He shakes her.*] May Buchanan!! I have
you!! I arrest you for –!! Oh Christ. [*He loosens his grip,
allows* MAY *to slump back into the boat. He reaches down
and touches her left breast.*] Christ and all the angels.
She's dead. [*Now he shoves her farther down, roughly.
Her body is no longer visible.* SEWARD *climbs out of the
rowboat.*]
[*Music: The second act tune, played like a lullaby,
harmonica, concertina or piano solo.*]
[SEWARD *turns and stares into the boat for a moment,
then takes a deep breath, and falls onto his knees. He
leans against the boat with one shoulder, and pushes it
down the sand and into the water. Breathing hard, he
continues pushing until the boat is actually afloat,
bobbing calmly, traveling outward – maybe only one end
of it is visible anymore.*] [SEWARD *falls back onto the
beach, and watches the little boat.*] That's it. Go on.
That's right. Farther. Go on, far away! Your sort's not
wanted here. Find some place, far away. Go on. No more
riches and French silk – no more smiles for you here,
my lady!! [*He drags himself to his feet, stares. He takes*
MAY's *pistol from his belt and throws it far away from
him, onto the sand. He looks out toward the bobbing,
disappearing rowboat again.*] Free now. Safe. Pure. [*He
picks up his buffalo coat and starts backing out, along the
beach, away from the water, dragging the coat with one
hand, never taking his eyes off the boat.*] Go on. Go on. Go
on. Go on. That's it. Go on. Go on. [*He disappears among
the trees and rocks.*]
[*Darkness. Seabirds, ships' horns and bells, as though
dawn were approaching.*]

Verses for the first act tune, 'Dear Maisie'

He said to me, on our first night,
He said to me, 'I love you!'
He said to me, 'Your eyes are bright,
Bright, bright as the stars above you!'

REFRAIN:
Sing doodle-oodle-oodle-doo,
Sing oodle-doodle-daisy!
Sing doodle-oodle-oodle-doo,
What happened next, dear Maisie?

He said to me, 'Your skin is pink,
Your cheeks are satin roses!'
He said to me, and gave a wink,
'Lass, let's at least rub noses!'

He said to me, 'Your eyes are blue
As pools both cool and shady!'
He said, 'I will be ever true,
And you will be my lady!'

He said to me, 'Now lay you down,
And I will lie quite near you!'
He said, 'Forbear to make a sound,
My mother must not hear you!'

He said to me, 'It is my will
To close your mouth with kisses!'
He said, 'My babes are sleeping still,
And please don't wake my missus!!'

John Murrell

Verses for the second act tune, 'The Bluest Eyes'

The bluest eyes,
So wise,
And yellow hair,
So fair,
The dearest heart,
And more:
Did he get what he came for?

The shelt'ring arm,
So warm,
The proudest gaze,
Ablaze,
The lips that all
Adore:
Did she get what she came for?

A skin so fine,
Divine,
A smile that beams
Bright dreams,
That thrill me to
The core:
But is it what I came for?

A blessed sleep,
So deep,
Then trumpets call
Us all
To Heaven's gol-
Den door:
But is it what we came for?

FARTHER WEST -- FIRST ACT TUNE: "DEAR MAISIE"

Murrell

Animated ♩ = 116

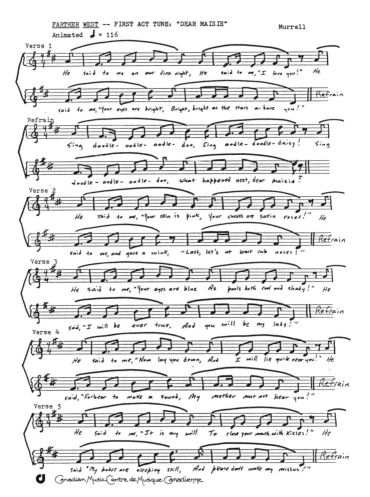

Verse 1
He said to me on our first night, He said to me, "I love you!" He said to me, "Your eyes are bright, Bright, bright as the stars a-bove you!"

Refrain
Sing doodle-oodle-oodle-doo, Sing oodle-doodle-daisy! Sing doodle-oodle-oodle-doo, what happened next, dear Maisie?

Verse 2
He said to me, "Your skin is pink, Your cheeks are satin roses!" He said to me, and gave a wink, "Lass, let's at least rub noses!"

Verse 3
He said to me, "Your eyes are blue As pools both cool and shady!" He said, "I will be ever true, And you will be my lady!"

Verse 4
He said to me, "Now lay you down, And I will lie quite near you!" He said, "Forbear to make a sound, My mother must not hear you!"

Verse 5
He said to me, "It is my will To close your mouth with kisses!" He said "My babes are sleeping still, And please don't wake my missus!"

FARTHER WEST -- SECOND ACT TUNE: "THE BLUEST EYES"
Gentle, quite slow ♩ = 80

Murrell

Verse 1
The bluest eyes, So wise, And yellow hair, So fair,
The dearest heart, And more: Did he get what he
came for?

Verse 2
The sheltering arm, So warm, The proudest gaze, Ablaze,
The lips that all a-dore: Did she get what she
came for?

Verse 3
A skin so fine, Divine, A smile that beams Bright dreams
That thrill me to the core: But is it what I
came for?

Verse 4
A blessed sleep, So deep, Then trumpets call Us all
To Heaven's gol---den door: But is it what we
came for?

Canadian Music Centre de Musique Canadienne

AIR FROM <u>MARITANA</u> -- for First Act of <u>FARTHER WEST</u>

V. Wallace

Cantabile

Words cannot scat-ter The thoughts we fear,

For though they flat-ter, They mock the ear.

Hopes will still de-ceive us With tearful cost, And

when they leave us The heart is lost, And

when they leave us The heart . . . . is

lost!

New World

a comedy

CREDITS:

New World was first presented in a co-production by the National Arts Centre Theatre Company, Ottawa (Producer, Andis Celms), and CentreStage, Toronto (Producer, Richard Ouzounian) in November, 1984, with the following cast:

BOB   William Hutt
LARRY   Michael Hogan
BET   Susan Wright
CARLA   Martha Henry
LINDA   Donna Goodhand
JEAN   Booth Savage
PETER   David Ferry

The play was directed by Robin Phillips, with set and costumes designed by Daphne Dare and Mr. Phillips, lighting by Michael Whitfield and Louise Guinand, and musical arrangements by Laura Burton; assistant to the designers was Arthur Penson.

CHARACTERS:

BOB, in his mid-fifties, originally from Great Britain, long transplanted to Canada

LARRY, his brother, in his early forties, more recently transplanted to the United States

BET, their sister, in her mid-forties, English

CARLA, Larry's wife, in her late thirties, American

LINDA, her daughter, young, American

JEAN, Bob's assistant, in his early forties, originally Francophone Canadian

PETER, Bob's apprentice, young, Anglophone Canadian

The action takes place on the southwest coast of Vancouver Island, British Columbia, Canada, in the course of a single day, late summer of the present year; the first scene and the last, at China Beach; the two scenes between, at China View, BOB's elegant large house near the beach.

There may be one interval, after the second scene.

for Robin

China Beach. Trees, sand and water.

*In the shade of a large beach umbrella, a canvas chair
and an easel, artist's paraphernalia for both water colour
and pencil sketch, have been set up.*

At one side, discarded clothes, towels, etc.

Music. BET *comes in, having a thoughtful smoke. She is
interrupted by distant laughing, splashing,* PETER *and*
LINDA *whooping it up in the ocean, off. She looks in the
direction of this noise, and starts to wave, then realizes
that* PETER *and* LINDA *have not seen her, are totally
involved in themselves. She cancels the wave.*

*She walks down a spit of sand, in another direction,
and stares out at the Pacific. She recites quietly,
singsong.*

BET	'Betty, Betty –
	In her petti' –
	Lives on ale – and stale confetti!'
	[*Much louder laughter and splashing from* LINDA *and*
	PETER, *now somewhat nearer.*]
	[BET *turns, looks in that direction, then drops her*
	cigarette and stamps it out. She hurries to the beach
	umbrella and seats herself, 'relaxed,' in the canvas chair.
	She begins to paint or sketch.]
	[LINDA *and* PETER *run in, glistening wet all over.*]
PETER	Morning!
	[*He chases* LINDA *near* BET.]
BET	You're dripping!
PETER	Sorry! We just couldn't resist!
LINDA	Morning, Bet.
PETER	Have you been here long?
BET	Hours and hours.
PETER	Like hell!
	[*He drapes himself, dripping, over a large dead tree.*
	LINDA *shakes or rubs herself dry.*]
LINDA	We were waiting for you. All of a sudden, it got really
	hot.
PETER	Well, quasi-hot.

99

LINDA	And Peter dared me to. So –
PETER	I knew she couldn't resist a dare.
LINDA	And I knew he'd be shocked as hell if I took him up on it! So – The water's still cold though. Even in the shallows. Even if the sun is quasi-hot.
PETER	Water that clean is always cold.
LINDA	Whatever! [*She lies on the sand, presents a rarely exposed part of her anatomy to the sunlight.*]
BET	Linda! Pet – what are you trying to –? What are you actually doing?
LINDA	It's the only way. Otherwise you get this really ugly white line, all along here. That bit just never gets any sun.
BET	Are you absolutely sure that bit – ought to get any sun?
LINDA	Why not?
BET	I'm not certain that God – or evolution – intended the human form for all-over tanning.
LINDA	Have you ever tried it?
BET	Me? I'd puff up like a toadstool! God's truth. One of those huge vermilion toadstools. With brown splotches! Eeek. – I must say that you look amazingly refreshed, baby Peter. Considering.
PETER	Considering what?
BET	Considering last night.
PETER	Jesus!
	[BET *and* LINDA *laugh.*]
PETER	I told Jean I couldn't handle cognac! Not after all that white wine! And the stuff with the fruit in it before.
LINDA	*Sangria.*
PETER	Jesus!
BET	Never mind. You're probably lucky to be alive. You moaned and whimpered all night long. I was listening at your bedroom door.
PETER	Like hell!
BET	God's truth. As though you were gripped by some terrible pain. Or some terrible lust. Which did you think it was, Linda? When you were listening? Middle of the night, outside Peter's door? Now, don't be embarrassed, pet! It's an obsession common to all us insomniacs, us unattached females and other nervous types. I

sometimes stand at a threshhold for hours. Just listening. Are they asleep? Are they talking to themselves, or to companions? Reciting poetry? Sobbing? Singing? Or just whimpering, like poor baby Peter? – Do you never recall your dreams, Peter?

PETER Never in public!

BET Too bad. It's what North America needs. More sensational novelists.

PETER I'm not a novelist.

BET You would be, if you could regurgitate your drunken nightmares. It's what they call talent.

PETER I'm a poet.

BET Ah! You regurgitate with a sense of rhythm! That's effete. No money in that.

PETER No real money in brown pencil seascapes either. Is there? Even when they include torsos as enticing as mine!

BET I fear you may be right. I blamed my first quarter-century of neglect on the post-war economic slump. But lately, I've become really apprehensive.
[*They laugh.*]
There! That's better! Much better. Now be still. [*She sketches.*]

LINDA I didn't know you were supposed to be any kind of writer. I thought you were studying photography. With Bob.

PETER I am, this summer. Nobody's hungry right now for slim volumes of verse. 'A picture's worth a thousand words.'

BET Or, in my esteemed elder brother's case, several thousand 'bucks,' words be damned. Words are effete!
[LARRY *comes in.*]

LARRY Here you are!

BET Here we are!

LARRY Isn't anybody besides me having lunch?

BET You won't have lunch, Larry. You'll have your customary handful of pills, your customary leaf of something green and gulp of water – then chatter away about your smashing new career, while our mouths are full. It's your one shot at a captive audience.

David Ferry (PETER), Michael Hogan (LARRY), Donna Goodhand (LINDA) and Susan Wright (BET).

LARRY   Morning, sis! Still in the same blue mood? [*He kisses her.*]

BET   This long 'blue period,' my life!

LARRY   Morning, Linda! Been for a splash? Morning, Peter! How's the head? – God, isn't it glorious?! Hot, actually hot! Practically California! Isn't it?

BET   [*To* PETER.] Can't you be still?

LARRY   Yes, siree! Virtually California! Or, at least, southern Oregon on a good day – bloody good day! You see those mountains there? Dark blue, across the straights? That's Washington! Washington state. Isn't it, Linda?
[LINDA *stands, puts on a few clothes, moves toward the water.*]
In fact, part of this island is actually south of Washington state – part of Washington state. Did you

realize that? Across the straits there, that's one country. And right here, not much more than spitting distance away, is quite another! Canada! Land of the caribou and polar bear! – Isn't Linda a knockout? Almost as much of a knockout as her mum! In fact, we're all knockouts this morning! That's the sort of mood I'm in! That lucky old sun is a knockout! The trees, the ocean! You're a knockout, Betsy. Young Peter's a knockout! Christ knows, I'm the most knocked-out of us all! God Almighty – glorious!! [*He has undressed to a minimal swimsuit.*]

LINDA   The surf's so rough this time of year. Nothing much but crab claws and dead sand-dollars. Jean claims he found a cowrie shell, down by the point yesterday. I told him, cowries can't live in water this cold. Probably fell off some tourist's charm bracelet.

BET   Or some cannibal's loincloth. What exactly is a cowrie?

LARRY   Who the hell cares? [*He stretches out on the sand.*]

LINDA   It's a snail.

BET   Peter –!

LINDA   A gastopod.

BET   – will you be still?!

LARRY   Don't nag, Betsy! The lad is young and full of zip!

BET   The lad is hungover. Aren't you, Peter? He was keening all night long, like a calf in the slaughterhouse. I was listening at his bedroom door.

LARRY   Good God!

BET   I was listening at your bedroom door too.

LARRY   Bullshit!

BET   You really must try not to behave like an American, Larry. We must all try not to behave like Americans.

LARRY   I am an American!

BET   Eeek.

LARRY   Now. So is Linda. She always has been.

PETER   Do you ever listen outside Bob's door?

BET   Of course. I'm everywhere! Bob doesn't make a sound, ever. He doesn't even breathe! You must've noticed, Linda?

LARRY   How in God's name could Linda notice? She only met him three days ago.

BET   Three days? Three nights! Look at her eyes. That

restless, somewhat rheumy stare. She's a mere novice, but the signs are clear to a kindred spirit. Insomniac! Door-listener!

[LINDA *laughs.*]

LARRY   Holy shit. After all these years, Bet, your bloody boldness can still take my breath away.

BET   Ah – that's a good sign!

LARRY   Carla was saying the same thing, just this morning.

BET   Carla hasn't known me 'all these years.'

LARRY   She was saying you can be pretty bloody bold.

BET   That hardly qualifies her as the world's keenest observer of human frailty. My boldness has been noted by people with scarcely one faculty intact.

[BOB *is heard, not yet seen.*]

BOB   Good morning, good morning!

BET   Speaking of whom ...

[BOB *comes in.*]

BOB   Good morning, everyone! What's funny? Am I unfastened? It's impossible to find all the – thingummies on these damned high-fashion things!

BET   'Good morning, everyone!' You should stop reading those newspaper pieces about your 'genial, expansive manner,' Bobby. It's turning you into a genial, expansive ass.

BOB   Oh, you know I never read anything. Jean sometimes reads me the good bits. Or – uh –

PETER   Peter.

BOB   Peter! I know. Peter. Good morning, Peter.

PETER   Did you sleep well?

BOB   Like the dead!

BET   What did I tell you?

[*They laugh.*]

BOB   What's funny? – Great God, Larry! Are you determined to burn yourself to oblivion?

LARRY   Bloody fantastic, isn't it? Practically California!

BOB   One can burn more quickly, more severely, under this slight haze that in undiluted sunlight! Didn't you know? Refracts the infrared – thingummies.

LARRY   So what? Peter and Linda and I are determined to get thoroughly refracted!

BOB   Peter and Linda haven't got our old-world tissue-paper skin. Look at Bet. She's no idiot.

BET   Contrary to rumour!

BOB   As a special favour, Lare: put your clothes on.
[LINDA *moves from the water to the beach umbrella.*]

LINDA   Look, Bet! Way out there! Those black and grey patches riding the waves? You think it could be migrating whales?

BOB   Not this time of year.

BET   I think it's a migrating oil slick.

BOB   Oh, shut up, Betsy! [*He laughs, sits.*]

LINDA   [*To* BET.] Look what I found. *Amphissa versicolor.* 'Joseph's Coat.' I didn't think these little guys ever wandered north of Big Sur.

BET   You may have noticed: all sorts of peculiar southern creatures are venturing northward this summer.

LINDA   That's a *lacuna carinata.* And that's a file. *Limatula – limatula* something – an oval clam.
[*Pause.*]

BOB   I dreamt I was late for a plane to Los Angeles. Do you ever have one of those dreams – so real – you're still walking around inside it, after you've been up for hours?

BET   Or even years?

BOB   I don't know why I was going to Los Angeles. To photograph somebody, I suppose.

LARRY   Everybody's in Los Angeles again, nowadays. Everybody.

BOB   I actually packed my shaving kit – packed the damned thing! – before I caught a glimpse in the mirror – and the ugly old bastard staring back at me said, 'We're not going to Los Angeles today, Bob. That was months ago.' Or 'months from now' – or something.
[LARRY *laughs.*]

LARRY   I dreamed I was late for a recording session once! Phoned this poor stupefied engineer and apologized for fifteen solid minutes, before he told me our lot wasn't even due in the studio for two solid weeks! Funny. I always dream at home, but never on holiday. I leave my anxieties behind! It's what you're supposed to do, isn't it?

BET   And isn't it cheering to know that all your little demons are waiting there to pounce, the instant you're back on familiar ground? Primed with weeks of pent-up hostility?

LARRY   Good God!

BOB   [*To* LARRY.] Is your bedroom comfortable at least? I never liked that east room. Nothing but scrub and magpies at the window.

LARRY   You ask me every morning, and every morning I tell you, 'It's more than comfortable, it's practically the Beverly Wilshire!' Then you ask Carla if it's at least liveable, and she tells you, 'It's more than liveable, Bob, it's practically the Beverly Wilshire!'

BET   '– practically the Beverly Wilshire!' It's practically mythic, Larry – the way you and your Yankee wife provide your own echo chamber! Of course, everyone knows America is where all the old myths went to live, when the post-war economic slump drove them out of Europe.

BOB   Mm ... true ... Post-what war? – And – uh – Linda? I suppose the wind must drive you mad, whistling around the windows, stuck out in that what-you-call-it as you are?

PETER   Cupola.

LINDA   I love the sound of wind! I can hardly sleep without it.

LARRY   Linda's what we call a romantic!

BET   All us unattached females and insomniacs are. Our only alternative is a life of crime. [*To* PETER.] Get up! Get up and go away. Go! You can't sit still!
[PETER *puts on clothes, moves away, lies down.*]

BOB   For God's sake! Was she trying to – was she sketching young –?

LARRY   Peter.

BOB   I know.

LARRY   You can sketch me if you want to, Betsy!

BET   Don't be silly. Put your trousers on.
[*She paints or sketches.* LINDA *moves toward the water again, wanders out briefly.*]

BOB   [*To* LARRY.] I want you and – I want you to have a nice time here.

LARRY   We are having a nice time.

106

BOB Did Jean take your breakfast order last night?

LARRY Yes.

BOB And it was delivered this morning?

LARRY Yes.

BOB On time?

LARRY Yes.

BOB And at least lukewarm?

LARRY Nice and hot.

BOB Not the orange juice?

LARRY No.

BOB Sometimes the orange juice is hot too! Enough to drive you mad.

LARRY The orange juice was nice and cold.

BOB Jean's been with me for years and years.

LARRY I know.

BOB Way back to when I was living in that – Slough of Despond – in – uh –

LARRY Montreal.

BOB I know. I suppose – after years and years – somebody like Jean – knows you better than you know yourself – inevitably – it becomes a sort of –

LARRY Marriage.

BOB Mm ... Not romantically. Not physically, of course.

LARRY No, no, no.

BOB But practically. Effectively. Efficiently. Sometimes that is all one really requires.

LARRY Sometimes.

  [CARLA, *not yet seen, is heard singing or humming, off.*]

BOB   Who's that? Your – uh –?

LARRY   Linda's mother. She's always singing, my better half! [*He calls, off.*] We're over here, Baby! Over here, Baby Duck!! [*To the others.*] Knockout eyes, but she can't see a damned thing without her specs!

[CARLA's *singing continues, off.* LINDA *wanders back in.*]

BOB   When I first came to this country – a billion years ago, give or take a few millennia – I felt obliged to capture it in paint. Just like you, Betsy. Sketch it, etch it – woodblock or water colour it. But eventually I realized how inappropriate our traditional media, our old world methods are – faced with this thrashing – raw – brash new world. So I bought my first camera!

PETER   A slightly-used Leica III-C, two interchangeable lenses, and an 'image-erecting Universal View Finder.'

BET   Give that lad a gold star!

[*They laugh.*]

BOB   Whitman. Whitman says, 'In the faces of men and women I see God.' But, of course, he didn't mean those weary old-world faces we grew up with. He meant this changing – this striving flesh. Which I've tried for all these years to capture with light and lens. Immediacy – people and their surroundings, seized, recorded in an instant – is the essential thing in a world so new – so rich and wild! 'In the faces of men and women.' He meant James Dean's face. Georgia O'Keefe's. Betty Bacall's! A new world in its new unvarnished look! Stubborn. Sexy. Not that old one, in its peeling mask. Which is all you'll ever capture with your chrome yellow and *chiaroscuro*, my dear Bet! The old world, squinting nervously at the new – buggering every single distinctive feature. The colour, drab. The light, ghastly. The perspective, hopelessly shallow and contrived! [*Pause.*]

BET   'In the faces of men and women I see God.' 'Men and women.' Does that mean God is a hermaphrodite? Or just that Walt Whitman was?

[*They laugh.* CARLA *comes in.*]

CARLA   Here you are!

BET   Here we are!

CARLA   Who would believe the weather could turn so glorious
        and sticky, and so fast? Before breakfast there was a
        breeze so strong the gulls were grounded. The water
        was like ice!

BET   Before breakfast?

        [LARRY *stands, moves to* CARLA, *kisses her.*]

LARRY   Yes, sir, that's my Baby! Swims two miles every morning,
        rain or shine! Is it any wonder she looks the way she
        does?

BET   Two miles?

CARLA   To tell the truth, I sometimes cheat just a tad on the last
        few hundred yards. [*She laughs, kisses* LARRY.]
        Sweetheart, put your shirt on. You're going to spoil my
        lunch.

LARRY   It's practically bloody California!

CARLA   Morning, Bet. What are you drawing?

BET   A crowd.

CARLA   Morning, Bob. I just love that east room. Those
        neighbourly birds at the window!

BOB   Magpies, I'm afraid.

CARLA   And beyond, for miles and miles, all that glorious –

BOB   Scrub.

CARLA   'This is the forest primeval –'

LINDA   Mother.

CARLA   'The murmuring pines and the hemlocks,
        Bearded with moss, and in garments green –'
        What comes next?

BET   'In the faces of men and women I see God.'

CARLA   I don't think so. Doesn't scan. Isn't anybody having
        lunch today?

PETER   I am!

CARLA   I snuck a peek at the kitchen. There was Jean, scrubbing
        and chopping and sautéing away, like a regular chef! I
        don't see how he can possibly surpass last night's
        pescado en vapor.

BET   Is that what it was? Well, Italy has hatched some queer
        ideas about what one does to a fish!

CARLA   It's Spanish actually. *Pescado*, not *pesce.*

LARRY   It must be a royal pain, hauling food all the way out
        here from – where? Victoria?

BOB	Some of it actually has to be brought from the mainland. Amazingly isolated, this peninsula.
BET	That's probably what attracts the crowd.
CARLA	And I do love the silence!
BET	The what?
CARLA	I know, it's not really silent, of course. There are the birds. The waves. 'The tide rises, the tide falls.' Human sounds too. Soft neighbourly footsteps in the corridor at night.
BET	What did I tell you? [*All but* CARLA *laugh.*]
BOB	What are we laughing at? – [*He gets to his feet.*] Let's go back! Everybody ready to go back?
BET	No. Not yet.
BOB	I might've know you wouldn't be.
BET	I'm going to stay and finish my sketches.
BOB	You know, I could cheerfully kill, at this moment, for a straight-up – thing – martini! Come on! [*He,* LARRY *and* PETER *go out, talking.*]
LARRY	Come on, Peter! Let's make our escape! [*To* BOB.] She was ogling him and scratching on that pad for a solid hour! Nagging him to be still. [CARLA *calls to* LARRY.]
CARLA	Sweetheart! Put your shirt on!
BOB	[*To* LARRY.] Well, you know our Betsy. She's got this 'master artist' thing under her skin – like a nasty rash! Simply refuses to listen to reason … [*They are gone.* CARLA *moves to* LINDA, *takes her hand.*]
LINDA	I'm going to stay awhile.
CARLA	Aren't you hungry?
LINDA	All we've done since we got here is eat.
CARLA	Isn't Jean fabulous? Practically Julia Child!
LINDA	I want to talk to Bet.
BET	Crikey.
CARLA	Well – don't stay too long. You don't get out as much as I do. Your skin's not properly toned up yet. Even with this haze, you can't be too careful.
BET	Beware the infrared thingummies! Isn't that right – Baby Duck?

[CARLA *gives her a look, then turns and goes out, singing or humming.*]

LINDA   Did you finish your sketch of Peter?

BET   No.

LINDA   Can I see?

[BET *shows her the sketch.*]

It's good! Exactly like him. Especially the hair! He's got nice hair.

BET   Anybody can do hair. [*She draws briefly.*] There. That's a face. Now you put in the hair.

[LINDA *draws.*]

Loosen your wrist! That's it. Don't think of separate strands. Think of tufts – shocks, locks, whatever. And think especially of light, playing across the crown, making it almost white. No need to waste your pencil there at all! That's it.

LINDA   You can't stand my mother. Can you?

BET   Well – I don't really know her that well. Do I? Yet.

LINDA   You're trying to be polite. You don't have to. Just say whatever you think.

BET   I think – I think it's not a sight to warm the cockles of my splotchety old British ego – you two, you and Mummy – Betty Bacall and Betty Bacall Junior, dashing through the spray! I have only to expose half an inch of flesh to that lucky old sun, I'll be richly rewarded with blisters and freckles and – freckles on my blisters! – No one else on earth has eyes like you Yanks! Especially the women.

LINDA   Our eyes? What are they like?

BET   I can't find the exact word. Fresh. Blank. Raw! That was Bobby's word, wasn't it? He's right about that at least. I always feel, if you took a European woman's eyes and peeled them with a paring knife, they would look like yours, your mother's. Wet. Open. [*She puts away her pencils, paints, etc.*]

LINDA	You've been living with your brother, how long? A couple of months?
BET	Bobby? I don't know. Seems longer.
LINDA	When Larry told us we were going to meet you at last, Mother didn't want to come.
BET	Well, she's nobody's fool.
LINDA	But I could hardly wait. To meet you especially!
BET	I suppose Larry had riveted you with tales of our seedy tweedy childhood? How I made 'impossible demands,' even as a child?
LINDA	Not really. Not much.
BET	I wouldn't give up my delusion of being a 'serious artist,' you see. That phrase was enunciated by our dear old Dad with scorn verging on nausea! 'Thinks she's gong to be "a serious bloody artist," our Bet does! Money for art school, twenty pounds per term!' Oh yes, our Bobbikins got all the same and more, years before. But that was different. 'Bob's got a man's head on his shoulders – very practical with it, don't you know? But Bet –! She hasn't a hope in hell!' – Prophetic words.
LINDA	What did your father do?
BET	Do? What could he do? Sneer and whine at me, and abuse dear old Mum.
LINDA	No, I mean, what did he – What was his profession?
BET	Ah! He professed tires. For automobiles and cycles. 'Pneumatic tyres!' he used to call them, with a wheeze of pride. The sort of profession in which you'd expect to find – I don't know – somebody from Michigan or Florida – but a hidebound old Brit? I don't believe Dad ever really felt 'at home' with it, over there. I suspect that's why Bobby and Larry migrated, first chance they got. To lose themselves amongst a whole continent of cheerfully aggressive tire salesmen, just like dear old Dad.
LINDA	But that's not why you came?
BET	Because I thought I'd 'fit in'? ... No. [*She starts out, leaving the beach umbrella, chair, painting paraphernalia.*]
LINDA	Aren't you going back to the house?
BET	No. Not yet.

LINDA	Where are you going?
BET	Down to the point. To look for cowrie shells. Or loincloths!
LINDA	What about all your stuff? Aren't you afraid somebody might snitch it?
BET	Who? Art thieves? A wandering band of water colourists?
LINDA	Do you want company?
BET	No. Thanks. Just the sea and me – and whatever else happens to be washed up.
LINDA	I'm glad we got a chance to talk.
BET	I talked. You listened.
LINDA	So? Good practice for a Yank, isn't it?
BET	Now, now, pet. Not fair. Satirize yourself, and you leave absolutely nothing for the old world to do.... Truth is, I had very little choice. About coming here, to plague poor old Bobby. The professor of pneumatic tyres' meagre bequest quickly dwindled to nothing. My entire roster of students for quick sketch and water colour comprised two excessively eager black youths, whose names I couldn't hope to pronounce. It was either the new world – or paupers' prison! I don't even know if there is a paupers' prison anymore. I mean, apart from the United Kingdom as a whole.... Then, one day, I found myself in conversation with the dead man from the flat upstairs. I assume he was dead. He never ate a morsel, to my knowledge. A hundred and fifty years old if he was a day. Professed to be reading Byzantine History on an allowance from his mother! He tried to warn me. 'Oh, it's all going!' he said, 'didn't you know? Doomed! Vancouver Island! Mexico too. California of course. Washington, Oregon, every scrap of Canada west of the Rocky Mountains! They might as well start erasing them from the maps! Continental drift, San Andreas Fault, the new Atlantis, read your Nostradamus!' He actually spoke like that – with the addition of a sepulchral quaver, which I will not attempt to reproduce. Clearly not a member of the mortal tribe. Even in dotty old England, one can distinguish between the eccentric and the supernatural. Sometimes.... It'll

113

come from miles away – out there! – a wave wider than the eyes can reach! So high it creates a new horizon halfway up the sky! And black! All the perennial filth with which we mortals have contaminated the immortal sea – oil slicks, industrial slime, carcasses of whales and seals and derelict steamers! – gathered into one Gargantuan black mouthful, and spat back in our astonished faces!! God's truth. My friend, the dead man, promised me! – Well, when I heard about that, and could look forward to waking up some morning – or turning round some afternoon – to see that! That at last! The last – last!! Then I began to look enormously forward to the new world! I ran to our branch library, discovered China Beach in the atlas, and pictured myself standing here – right here! – welcoming that wave! No doubt the old world will have its trauma too. But nothing half so obliterating, exhilarating – ! The monster tides at Penzance will seem like the swirl at the foot of your bath – compared to our black wave! [*She goes out along the beach.*]

LINDA 'No one else on earth has eyes like you Yanks!' 'Fresh. Wet. Open.' – I think I'm in love! [*She hurries out after* BET.] [*Pause.*] [*Music.* CARLA *and* JEAN *come in, laughing.*]

CARLA I swear to you – they were right here a moment ago! I could just make them out, from up at the house. And there's no mistaking that umbrella.

JEAN And now the others can probably just make us out – from the house. Maybe they can even see where Bet and Linda have gone. From up there. But I can't. I don't see a living soul!

CARLA I see you ... Jean! ... [JEAN *smiles, then turns and calls, off.*]

JEAN Bet ...?!

CARLA Bet! Linda ...?! – Obviously out of earshot. Out of sight, out of ... Probably gone for a long walk. [*She looks around.*] You know, I don't really think anybody could see you – from up at the house. Not if you were sitting down, quite still. [*She sits.*] Not even if they were glued to the windows.

[JEAN *laughs, moves nearer.*]

CARLA I've never known anything like it! This weather! This fragile haze which – makes it even hotter. Stickier. Magically. Nothing at all like California!

JEAN You hardly touched your lunch. Did you try the salmon? The *'Coho en croute'*? Fresh this morning, from north of here, up the coast.

CARLA You know, I can't put it out of my mind. That – What you were playing for me this morning. On the stereo. You were so right about that melody. It has phenomenal – shape!

[JEAN *touches her. She sings or hums.*]

Andante mosso moderatamente ♩. = 50

JEAN I only regret we were interrupted – before the first act finale. *'Un viso d'angelo!'* 'The face of an angel!' [*He takes something, wrapped in wax paper, from his pocket.*] I brought your dessert. It's not healthy, you know, to miss your dessert. – Almond macaroon. Marzipan inside! [CARLA *eats it rapidly from his hands.*]

CARLA I think I'm in love!

[*They laugh, then sing or hum together.*]

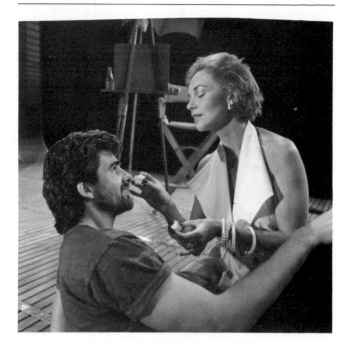

Booth Savage (JEAN) and Martha Henry (CARLA).

*China View: A large, modern room. A vast window
overlooking the beach. Many photographs of the famous
and near-famous. Modern stereo, TV, video tape
player/recorder.*

    JEAN *and* CARLA *are listening, entranced, to the act one
finale of* La Fanciulla del West.

    LARRY *and* PETER *come in.*]

LARRY   – exactly what I'm saying! Exactly what I'm saying! Even
if you came in on the ground floor, so to speak! And
there's at least two totally different directions from
which you could do just that! Sit down there now – take
a gander at this thing – and tell me what you think!
[*He turns the video player and TV on, shoves a cassette
into the player.* PETER *sits, watches the TV.*]

116

There's the whole technological end of the thing –
twenty-four, thirty-eight, forty-eight tracks – sky's the
limit! Then there's the marketing thing – my thing! –
which I literally have to run like your proverbial rabbit
to keep up with! I can't see why anybody your age –!
[*Loud rock music erupts from the TV.*]
– with your varied interests and educational
background –! All right! See what I mean?

JEAN   *Addio*, Puccini! [*He moves to the stereo, stops the
Puccini record.*]

CARLA   [*To* LARRY.] Sweetheart?

LARRY   [*To* PETER.] Well? What do you think?

PETER   I – don't know –

CARLA   Sweetheart?

PETER   Let me just get used to it for a second, okay?

LARRY   I can't see why anybody your age would be interested in
anything else!

PETER   Really?

LARRY   That's the future you're watching! And listening to! Eyes
and ears – bombarded – invaded! – now! –together! A
single receiving organ, a single sensual response!

CARLA   Larry!
[*He turns to her.*]

LARRY   Sweetheart? Hi! Isn't this great? [*To* PETER.] 'Sensual
synthesis!' That's a phrase that actually came out of our
office, as a matter of fact! Now everybody's using it!

CARLA   Larry –

LARRY   Another five years and the LP record will be extinct!!

CARLA   Sweetheart?!
[*He turns to her.*]

LARRY   Baby Duck?

CARLA   Come here, please.

LARRY   I was just telling Peter all about our complexes, our
equipment, our sales thrust! [*He goes to her, gives her a
quick kiss.*]

CARLA   Sweetheart, have you seen Linda?

LARRY   This morning. On the beach.

CARLA   But not since?

LARRY   No. I don't know. – So, Pete?! What do you think?

PETER   Is it all like this?

LARRY	All? Oh Christ, no! Our product is absolutely unique! Look at that colour!
PETER	No, I mean, is it like this – all the way through?
LARRY	What do you want?! The whole tape's only seventeen and a half minutes! Three songs, seventeen and a half minutes!
CARLA	Larry –?!
LARRY	And we just got started! You literally would not believe the growth potential!
CARLA	Sweetheart, obviously you didn't notice – when you came in –!
LARRY	[*To* PETER.] Not just here and in Canada!
PETER	This is Canada.
CARLA	When you came into the room just now –!
LARRY	South America is literally itching for a quality product! Are you ready for that?! Sweden, Germany – West Germany, of course! Italy, even North Africa! And I fell into it! Literally fell onto my out-of-touch English ass –! [CARLA *moves to the stereo/TV/video equipment.*] – in the middle of four hundred, like I told you, maybe even four hundred and fifty, minimum per –!! What happened? [*The rock video has stopped.*] I told Bobby his bloody equipment's not worth a tinker's fart!
CARLA	I shut it off, sweetheart.
LARRY	You did?
CARLA	When you burst in here just now, without a civil word or look, we were already engaged in listening!
LARRY	You were?
CARLA	Jean and I.
LARRY	Jean and –?
CARLA	That's Jean. [JEAN *waves.*]
LARRY	You and Jean were –?
CARLA	Listening.
JEAN	To Puccini.
LARRY	Puccini?
JEAN	*Girl of the Golden West!* [LARRY *shoves the cassette back into the video player.*]

CARLA Don't turn that on again! Please, darling. – A little more
Puccini, Jean? Please?

LARRY Sweetheart –

CARLA *Girl of the Golden West!* I was born just outside Denver!
Did I already tell you that? God's Country!

LARRY Darling –

CARLA [*To* LARRY.] I don't understand how you can brush right
past people! As if we'd ceased to exist! As if we were
automatic doors at a supermarket, which just whoosh
aside to let you pass!

LARRY Whoosh? Are you speaking to me?

CARLA It must be a habit you acquired in your youth. Over
there, where there are so many more people, so much
less time and space!

JEAN But hardly any supermarkets.
 [CARLA *laughs.*]

LARRY Don't put that on again! Jean?

PETER Is Bob in the dark room? Does anybody know?

CARLA Sweetheart! You're making everyone very nervous.

LARRY I am?

CARLA Come and sit down. Please? You want some fruit, or a
Perrier or something? I worry about you. Did you take
your pills? – We were just trying to have a – moment,
you see? Jean and I. A nice relaxing – moment!

JEAN With Puccini.

CARLA With wonderful Signore Puccini!

LARRY And I was just – Peter asked about my work. He says he
knows there's lots of money, but is there any real future
in it!

PETER Actually all I said was –

CARLA It's a question of atmosphere, darling! No, something
even more elusive than atmosphere. The passing
tranquil moment! Of course, we all want to hear about
your work, your quality product. Tonight at dinner, why
not? Or this weekend? When the mood, when the
occasion is right. 'Know your moment!' Isn't that what
Georgie Jessel used to say?

LARRY I wasn't attempting to – be Georgie Jessel, sweetheart! I
was just explaining –

CARLA You miss my point! Your product was not designed for

tranquility! Which is what Jean and I are after. *Capsice?* Puccini, on the other hand –

LARRY Screw Puccini!

[*Pause.*]

PETER I think I'll check the dark room! Just in case.

[*He hurries out.* LARRY *glares at* CARLA. JEAN *moves to the window, looks out.*]

CARLA What is wrong with you?

LARRY With me? Good God! You're the one who's been – for the past three days – more than a bit – desultory.

CARLA Desultory?

LARRY Desultory!

CARLA You don't know what that word means.

LARRY You bloody well have been! More than a tad – desultory.

CARLA I didn't want to come.

LARRY We had to come. Bob invited us –

CARLA You had to come.

LARRY – to see Bet settled in.

CARLA You must've known that Bet would settle in overnight! Like the London fog.

LARRY She's my sister.

CARLA And you can't bear the sight of her.

LARRY That's not true.

JEAN There they are now.

LARRY That's a damned lie!

CARLA What did you say?

LARRY I said that's a –

CARLA Jean! Didn't you say something?

JEAN Linda and Bet. There they are. On their way up. [*He points out the window.*]

CARLA From the beach? They'll be as red as lobsters! [*She moves to the window.*]

JEAN Yes. They look almost like lobsters. From up here, don't they? Crawling up from the beach!

LARRY Excuse me –

CARLA [*To* JEAN.] Want some? It's delicious, but very sticky!

JEAN Mmm.

[*They eat fruit.*]

CARLA Linda with bare shoulders! And not even a hat!

JEAN What have they got? What are they carrying?

LARRY	Excuse me, please –
CARLA	They're carrying something? Oh Lord, not another truck load of shells and fish skeletons!
JEAN	I don't think so.
LARRY	Excuse us –
CARLA	You should see her room at home!
JEAN	Look at them. They're being very careful with it, whatever it is.
CARLA	Linda looks so young, in the outdoors. Like a schoolgirl!
JEAN	Almost as young as you do.
CARLA	Liar! Why is it that every single man I know – who was raised on a romance language – is so smooth, so expert, when it comes to – flattery and –?
LARRY	Excuse–us –one–flaming–bloody–minute!!
	[*Pause.*]
CARLA	Sweetheart?
LARRY	Excuse us, please. Jean? My wife and me? My wife and I want to talk!
CARLA	Darling? First you accuse me of being desultory and then –!
LARRY	Bullshit, Carla! [*To* JEAN.] My wife and I – maybe you can tell – are in the middle of a rather – intimate conversation? If you could please excuse us? [JEAN *smiles at him, and goes out.*] Thank you. *Merci.* [CARLA *moves to the stereo, starts the Puccini record.*] Don't do that. – Carla? [*She stops the record.*]
CARLA	You're all – so – desultory, your family! I can't breathe here, I can't acclimatize myself in this house! It's like I'm confronted by – by an alien species!!
LARRY	Good God.
CARLA	Seriously! Sweetheart. I'm swimming around and around and around inside a very small fish bowl! But most of my species, most of the normal fish, are out there! Swimming free in the open air, like they're meant to! I don't know. You're such a – an exotic breed! Bet – and Bob – just lie there – on the murky bottom – waiting for me or Linda to swim past!
LARRY	So they can gobble you up?

CARLA   Seriously! I've never known anybody, never even read
        about anybody, quite like your sister.

LARRY   Bet is a perfectly ordinary, run-of-the-mill embittered
        English spinster – and failed painter.

CARLA   And Bob –!

LARRY   That's different. Bob's a genius, or the nearest thing to it.
        Enough of a genius to get out while he was young.
        Young enough to change, make a new life for himself!

CARLA   It's got nothing to do with genius! We just don't have –
        families which – interrelate like yours! Families! In the
        United States!

LARRY   Oh God, not another installment of 'our Yankee
        heritage'! I studied all that hoop-la before I put in for
        citizenship.

CARLA   There! See? You sound just like your sister!

LARRY   Bullshit.

CARLA   I'm not setting myself up as superior, sweetheart. Not in
        any way. Just different. From a different – planet, I
        almost think, sometimes! – I simply don't comprehend
        the old world. I guess I never will.

LARRY   Except for wonderful Signor Puccini, of course.

CARLA   That's not the same.

LARRY   And always excepting Jean, your pet pastry chef!

CARLA   Puccini doesn't belong to the old world! He belongs to
        the whole world!

LARRY   And what whole does dear little Jean belong to?

CARLA   Jean is French –

LARRY   He's Canadian!

CARLA   Same thing! – Practically!

LARRY   What is it exactly about him? Tell me. You can always
        tell me everything. – Is it his cooking? They all cook, you
        know. Every bloody clever one of them! – Is it just the
        music? They all get into Mozart and opera and all that.
        It's not genuine sophistication. They grow up with it! It's
        just – conditioning. Truly! Upper class French-Canadian
        snob conditioning. – Or is it – is it just the bloody sexy
        accent? The way the consonants roll off his tongue?!
        What in hell is it?!
        [*She looks directly at him.*]
        Oh. – I see! [*He moves away from her.*] I expected –

better of you – Baby Duck! Call me an out-of-touch old
world asshole – I really expected – better of you!
[*Pause.*]

CARLA   I'm not in love with him! I'm not even attracted to him.
You think I'm attracted to him. I'm not even seriously
attracted to him!
[*Pause.*]
[*She suddenly bursts into tears.* LARRY *stares at her a
moment, then quickly moves to the stereo, starts the
Puccini record.*]

LARRY   I certainly didn't intend to suggest – [*He looks around
nervously, then suddenly points out a photograph.*] Hey!
Hey, isn't that – what's-his-name? Buster Keaton!
[*She looks up.*]

CARLA   It's – Eugene O'Neill!! [*More tears.*]

LARRY   Right! That's who I meant! Christ, he's been dead for
donkey's years, hasn't he? Eugene O.? Bobby must've
snapped that one soon after he came over. Back when
he worked for – what's-its-name – the magazine? – I'm
not nervous! Or – Good God! How bloody 'old hat,' 'old
world' do you think I am?! [*He moves to her.*] I never
minded you having friends! Did I? Just friends? I think
Jean's – lovely. I always thought so. I know – he's a very
– sexy man. And needing a large – warm – circle of
friends – is a perfectly normal part of being – American
–!
[*She pulls away from him. He moves to the stereo, stops
the Puccini record.*]
I'm proud! You want me to be proud of what I do? I
wouldn't bloody well be doing it, if it weren't for you! It
was totally your idea – inspiration! And mostly your
investment! So I'm bloody well proud! I want to show
young Peter how proud I am! So bloody proud and
enthusiastic I don't happen to notice you, and 'Julia
Child,' and the *Girl of the Golden Frigging West*!! It's not
a capital offense! Not to notice!!

CARLA   Maybe it ought to be!!
[*He moves to the video player/TV, and starts the rock
cassette, very loud.* CARLA *turns away from him.*]
[LINDA *comes in, carrying a very large sphere of*

123

Donna Goodhand (LINDA), Martha Henry (CARLA) and
Susan Wright (BET).

translucent blue glass. She is followed by BET, *who is
exhausted, red in the face.* LARRY *sees them, moves to the
video player, and turns the rock video off.*]

BET	Aaaaahh!
CARLA	What's that thing? Where were you two?
BET	How many times have you ingested that mess of musical pottage,Lare?
LARRY	I was in the studio when they made it.
BET	Eeek. [*She fixes herself a drink.*]
LARRY	You wouldn't call it a mess, if you could see its projected revenue!
BET	Oh yes, I would.
CARLA	[*To* LINDA.] What is that?
LINDA	It's Bet's. She caught it.
BET	God's truth. Or rather, it caught me. By surprise! You

know how blind I am, and it's as blue as – I was going to say 'as the sea,' but the sea's not actually blue, is it? Not anymore. At any rate, there I was, sloshing about in the puce and garbage-bag green sea – when it bumped right into me and said 'Hello' – in Japanese!

CARLA   What is it?

LINDA   A float.

LARRY   A what?

LINDA   Float.

CARLA   What's it supposed to do?

LINDA   Float.

CARLA   Everybody around here is starting to sound just like you, Bet!

BET   There's a cheering thought.

CARLA   Let me see it. [*She takes the sphere.*] Exquisite. Blown glass. I knew a glass blower once. From La Jolla. She died, tragically young, of lung cancer. Her doctor swore there was no connection between glass-blowing and lung cancer. But I couldn't help suspecting –
[BET *takes the sphere from her.*]

BET   It's a Japanese fishing-net float! They get washed up, from time to time – as who doesn't – on good old China Beach. Jean has five or six of them on the bookshelf in his room. You must've noticed, Carla? In a variety of decorator colours.
[LARRY *looks at* CARLA. BET *steps between them, shows* LARRY *the sphere.*]
Look! So frail. So delicate. Yet able to survive – the sea! Makes you wonder, doesn't it?
[*She moves to* LINDA, *hands her the sphere.*]
Makes you – re-think, re-examine. Almost makes you believe in something! – Jap glass blowers, I guess!
[*She and* LINDA *laugh.*]

CARLA   [*To* LARRY.] That's what you call 'perfectly ordinary'? 'Run-of-the-mill'?

LARRY   What's wrong with you, Bet?

LINDA   Oh, leave her alone! Can't you understand, she's nervous. Expecting her black wave, any minute now?

BET   Ssshh.

LARRY   Expecting her what?!

125

CARLA Do you ever get the feeling you're some poor old movie actor who just wandered onto the wrong set?
[BOB *comes in.*]

BET Speaking of whom ...

BOB What's that thing?

LINDA A float.

BOB Ah! For God's sake. – Where's – uh – ?

CARLA Jean?

BOB No.

LINDA Peter?

BOB Peter.

LARRY In the dark room. Looking for you.

BOB Middle of the afternoon? What would I be doing in the dark room?

BET Hiding from me.

BOB Right. Right you are! [*He goes out.*]

LARRY Betsy –?

BET Laresy?

LARRY What did you mean?

BET Mean?

LARRY Just now. You asked Carla if she had noticed Jean's bookshelf.

CARLA Sweetheart –

LARRY We've only been here three days. What in God's name would Carla be doing, sniffing around Jean's bookshelf?

CARLA Honestly! You're not going to start interrogating –

LARRY Bullshit, Carla! [*To* BET.] Well?
[JEAN *comes in.*]

BET Here you are!

JEAN Here I am.

CARLA [*To* LARRY.] Jean showed me his collection of shells and driftwood and fishing-net floats yesterday afternoon, sweetheart.

LARRY Then how come you didn't know what that thing is?!
[*He points to the sphere.*]

CARLA Don't be silly. Jean's are much smaller than that.

BET Nearly everybody's are.

CARLA I was telling Jean about Linda's heap of oceanic trivia – so it was perfectly natural for him to invite me to – Will you please stop behaving like Grendel's Mother?!

126

JEAN	Who is Grendel's Mother?
LARRY	Who the hell cares?! It's from some bloody – American poem! [CARLA *laughs.*]
BET	Oh good. I thought she meant me.
LARRY	Would you please – Linda – take that damned thing to your room?!
LINDA	It's not mine. It's Bet's.
CARLA	He's just trying to get rid of you, angel.
LINDA	There's no need to. I haven't the faintest idea what's going on.
LARRY	Jean?! *Mon ami?* Come over here and look me straight in the eye. Will you do that for me?!
CARLA	I think poor old Larry got too much sun this morning!
LARRY	Better too much sun than – than bloody peaches and Puccini!!
BET	I love this sort of conversation.
JEAN	Why don't you come over here, Larry? The light's much better over here.
LARRY	Jesus-loving-Christ!! How can you all live with yourselves and be so – bloody desultory?!
CARLA	He doesn't know what that word means!
LARRY	[*To* JEAN.] Listen to me! You will bloody well hop over here for a minute and look me in the frigging eye!! [BOB *comes in, followed by* PETER.]
BOB	What's all the bloody shouting? [*Pause.*]
CARLA	I'm going for a nap!
LARRY	You try to leave this room, I swear to God I'll flatten you!!
BOB	Larry! What on earth?! [*Pause.*]
LARRY	Go on then! Go for your damned nap! Who the hell cares?
BOB	I leave a bevy of well-fed lethargic house guests, and return to a swarm of carnivorous fish!
LARRY	Fish? Shit! [BET *laughs.*]
BOB	What's funny?
BET	I haven't the faintest idea! Linda and I are virginal onlookers, immemorial caryatids observing the chaos.

Also baby Peter. Can you have a male caryatid?

[CARLA *goes out.* JEAN *follows.*]

LARRY   Where's he going?!

JEAN   To the dark room!

LARRY   Oh, of course! No play on words intended?!

BOB   [*To* JEAN.] Will you check those drums of solvent again? Something smells.

LARRY   It certainly does!!

[JEAN *goes out.*]

BOB   [*To* LARRY.] What is wrong with you?!

LARRY   Will everybody stop asking me that?! Please?! – It's perfectly – childishly obvious! If you weren't all so bloody – childish!!

BOB   What in God's name are you talking about?!

[LARRY *moves away from the others.* PETER *moves to* LINDA, *takes the blue sphere from her.*]

PETER   I never saw one this big before. Where'd you find it?

LINDA   It's Bet's. Down by the cove.

PETER   Large or small cove?

LINDA   I didn't know there was more than one.

PETER   The large one is miles further. The road doesn't pass anywhere near it. I go there when I really want to disappear.

LINDA   Sounds perfect! You know the large cove, Bet?

[BET *smiles at her.*]

PETER   There's even a sort of grotto. Well, a quasi-grotto. Something magic about it. Quasi-magic. If you want to believe badly enough! You have to be careful though, or the tide traps you inside.

LINDA   And then what?

PETER   You drown, I guess.

[*They laugh.*]

Want to go have a look?

LINDA   Sure! Sure, why not?

[*She glances at* BET *again, then starts out after* PETER.] What is it exactly that makes your quasi-grotto quasi-magic? [*She takes the blue sphere from him.*]

PETER   Hard to say. The quasi-privacy maybe. The quasi-danger.

LINDA   Quasi-quasi-quasi! The call of the Canadian wild!

PETER   Well, the quasi-wild!
        [*Laughing, they go out, taking the sphere with them.*]
BET   I can't remember – can you, Bobby? – when we were
        young enough to toss aside a blistering morning
        hangover – be chipper as stoats again by mid-
        afternoon?
BOB   Remember? Of course I can. I'm still young enough!
        [BET *laughs, fixes herself another drink.*]
BET   'Bobby, Bobby,
        Found a hobby,
        Rode it 'till his knees were knobby!'
        Remember that?
BOB   No.
BET   Oh yes you do! – Our Larry is afraid his Carla is having it
        off with your Jean.
BOB   Having it –?
BET   Off. Carla and Jean.
BOB   I haven't heard that expression in twenty years.
BET   Sometimes I wonder whether you've done it in twenty
        years.
BOB   Mm. Is that so? At least I would have some excuse. My
        calling. My compulsion, my work. You wouldn't
        understand.
BET   You mean taking snapshots?
BOB   Snap –?! Is that –? [*He points.*] – what you call a
        'snapshot'?!
BET   Not really. It lacks the candour and spontaneity of a
        genuine snapshot. Shall I lend you my Instamatic?
BOB   'Betty, Betty,
        In her petti',
        Lives on ale and stale confetti!'
        Remember that?
BET   No.
BOB   Oh yes you do! [*He moves to* LARRY.] Carla and Jean are
        not having it off. I promise you.
LARRY   A lot you'd care.
BOB   Of course I'd care! Jean's been with me for years and
        years.
        [BET *laughs.*]
        What's funny?!

LARRY	I didn't even want to come! Linda and her mother insisted. They were dying to meet you!
BET	And they've been dying ever since.
BOB	Oh, shut up, Bet! [*To* LARRY.] Don't you suppose I'd know, if Jean were involved? With anyone? After all these years? Don't you suppose I'd at least suspect it – virtually before he did?
LARRY	No! No, that's just more of your – quasi-mystical codswallop! You think you can see right through the rest of us, like we're – some damned Jap fishing-net floats! You always thought so!
BOB	For God's sake!
LARRY	It's true! Even when we were kids, you'd climb up onto your high horse – to predict what'd become of all of us! Remember, Bet? Not just you and me and Mum and Dad. Every-bloody-body!
BOB	Nine times out of ten, I was right.
LARRY	Get serious!
BOB	I predicted you'd leave home, less than a decade after my departure!
LARRY	Of course I left home! I was twenty-four bloody years old!
BOB	I predicted you'd end up in North America.
LARRY	Where else was I going to end up?
BOB	Australia.
LARRY	Get serious!
BOB	I predicted our Betsy would sit and stew on the uncongenial family hearth – till she was literally, legally evicted! I predicted she'd never quite made a go of it with her – antediluvian water colours and – pointillist doodles!
LARRY	You knew she wasn't really good enough! Dad knew that! Mum too, though she never admitted it. Everybody knew it!
BET	Ah, but I knew it first.
LARRY	Of course, you did predict Mum and Dad would die, when they got old!
BOB	I predicted Mum would be the first to go!
LARRY	So did the whole flipping neighbourhood! She greeted each new day with a cough like flaming Krakatoa!!

130

BET   Larry!

LARRY   Why do you make me say things like that?! I don't want
        to talk anymore!
        [*He moves away from them.* BOB *follows.*]

BOB   Listen to me! Lare? No, listen! The moment you set foot
        in this house, three days ago, I could see that you and –
        Carla! – were not completely congenial.

BET   Did this have anything to do with the spiked leash by
        which she was dragging him?

BOB   [*To* LARRY.] I could see that you and Carla will never be
        really happy!

LARRY   What a bloody-minded thing to say!

BOB   But it's got bugger-all to do with Jean!! Trust me. That is
        just your compulsive old-world hunger for – a
        scapegoat!

LARRY   My what?!

BOB   A handy excuse for your – predetermined, self-inflicted
        unhappiness! Nothing to do with Jean! Whatsoever!! –
        Listen, carefully! I know Jean. I know him! I – have –
        photographed – Jean!
        [*Pause.*]

LARRY   I need a sedative. Doesn't anybody have a sedative?

BET   I don't use sedatives. I paint.
        [*Pause.*]

BOB   Of course, the fact that you and – Carla will never be
        happy is no reason why you shouldn't have a long and
        interesting life together! If that's the sort of life you want.
        Everything is possible – in this thrashing – raw – free –
        thingummy!
        [*Pause.*]

BET   Amazing. – Well, Lare, I might hazard a guess – what
        Bobbikins is trying to tell us is: nobody is having it off
        with Jean ... except him.
        [*Pause.*]

LARRY   Except who?

BOB   That is the oldest rag of unfounded rumour on earth!

BET   Bob and Jean.

LARRY   Bob and –?

BET   Unthinkable, isn't it? In our family! That's why I've
        always thought it must be true.

131

LARRY	Not – romantically? Physically?
BOB	God, here we go! Here come those tired old – fears, sneers and jeers! 'Poor old Bobby should've got married, shouldn't he? Some undemanding, unflappable, unenlightened female – who signs her name to Christmas cards – and cooks a thoroughly mediocre, indisputably heterosexual pot roast!!' – Marriage, however degraded, is the one shield which Bobby and other old farts of his general sort bear – against sniggering supposition! 'Unmarried and creative, eh? Unmarried and dresses well? He must be – one of those!' I simply never had a spare moment to – go through the motions of matrimony! I was perfecting my work – my second sight! Yes, Bet – that is precisely, irrevocably what it was – what it is!! For all these centuries, my relentless pursuit of the new world – exploding, crawling with life! – has left me peculiarly vulnerable to – half-dead journalists! And various filthy-minded old tarts! ... I daresay I should've got married. A token spouse. Sometimes that is all one really requires. [*Pause.*]
LARRY	You mean to tell me – people – not just Bet, but people! – actually think that you and Jean –?
BOB	Why not? What else have most of those lightless Munchkins got to occupy their so-called minds?! Scavenging for slimy, shiny bits in the dungheap of libidinous speculation! Me and Jean! Me and young – Peter too! Me and you, Lare! Why not? Me and the bleeding Prime Minister!!
BET	'The bleeding Prime Minister and I.'
LARRY	– You mean – the Prime Minister was –?!
BOB	Me and Albert Schweitzer no doubt! Before the old sod expired, in an agony of unnatural rapture!!
LARRY	Albert Schweitzer –?! [*The sudden unmistakable music of shattering glass, not far off.* BOB, BET *and* LARRY *turn and stare in that direction.* PETER *comes in, bearing large fragments of the blue glass sphere.*]
PETER	Sorry. It wasn't my fault! It wasn't really Linda's either. We just had – different plans. I wanted to take it with us

– sent it back where it came from! I got excited,
picturing it – washing up on the other side, over there!
Japan. Or on a real China beach. Months, maybe years,
from now. Intact, unchanged by all our attentions – but
amazingly well-traveled! That should only happen to all
of us, eh? ... Sorry.

[BET *looks at the fragments, then turns away, tears in her eyes.*]

BET   The sea be damned! One can always depend – can't
one? – on the young! To wake one up, and finish one off!
To fracture – whatever one still has, that's not already
fractured?!

PETER   I said I'm sorry! What the hell – crucify me! I got excited!
I'm a poet.

[*Music.* LINDA *comes in, weeping, with more fragments of the sphere.*]

---

*China View: the same large room, but now a vast array of
expensive, complicated photographic equipment has
been set up, here and there, all around.*

JEAN *and* CARLA *are listening to the* Finale Ultimo *of* La
Fanciulla del West. BOB *watches, irritably, from one side.
Music concludes.*

CARLA   God, I'm hungry! [*To* JEAN.] Aren't you hungry?

BOB   No. – Was that the end? The actual end? – Good! [*He
moves among his photographic equipment.*]

CARLA   God! Puccini! [*She sings.*]

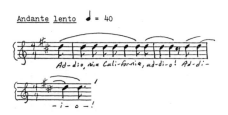

CARLA   [*To* JEAN.] I want you to write down the artists and the number of that album. Do you mind? There's a store on Doheny that has absolutely every record ever made! [*She sings.*]

[*A brilliant flash of light.*]

CARLA   What was that?! – [*To* BOB.] You crafty old devil! You took my picture!

BOB   No, I didn't.

CARLA   Here I sit – my mouth wide open – and I haven't put my face on for three days!

JEAN   You look terrific.

CARLA   What are you going to call that one? 'Woman Going To Pieces Over Puccini?'

BOB   I call them 'photographs.'

CARLA   I'd never have suspected you for – an image thief! That's what a savage from New Guinea would call you – a Papuan!

BOB   I don't know any savages. Do I, Jean?

JEAN   Not from New Guinea.

CARLA   They're absolutely terrified of cameras! They believe if you steal a person's image, you steal his soul!

BOB   In a way, they're right.

CARLA   Oh – it makes me feel all sort of – runny inside! My very soul, trapped inside the Bwana's little black box! [*She taps the camera.*]

BOB   Don't do that!

JEAN   She won't hurt it.

BOB   How do you know?

CARLA   So what's the procedure? You offer me all existing prints, plus the negative, for a cool million? Otherwise, you expose my unkempt, Puccini-drenched soul – where? *The National Enquirer*?! Whereupon I douse you and your entire studio with developing fluid, then casually drop a lighted match –?!

BOB   Please – I'm sorry – I'm afraid –

JEAN	Carla.
BOB	I did not take you picture, dear heart. I took my own. I do it all the time.
CARLA	– Are you serious?
JEAN	He's planning his autobiography. In the form of a series of self-portraits! Much to his publisher's dismay.
BOB	You leave my publisher out of this! He's been wrong before.
JEAN	He's not wrong this time.
CARLA	So you really didn't –? That wasn't me, just now? Scout's Honour?
BOB	Scout's Honour! Whatever that is.
JEAN	You see? Your soul is intact.
CARLA	I see.
BOB	[*To* JEAN.] I've made more than one publisher's reputation, not to say fortune! Publishers are always twenty years behind the times.
JEAN	Exactly. They're perfectly in step with public taste!
BOB	You're just a snob, that's your problem.
CARLA	Why didn't you? – Bob?
BOB	Pardon me?
CARLA	Why didn't you? Take my picture?
BOB	Could you possibly – shift, dear heart? Just a smidgen? That way? I told you –
CARLA	I know! You snapped yourself. What I'm wondering is: in the three, three whole days since we arrived, why haven't you tried, even once, to snap me?!
BOB	Sorry. You're still in the shot. Another inch and a half? That way!
CARLA	No!
JEAN	I guess I should start supper. [*He stands.*]
CARLA	[*Turns to* JEAN.] I'm not willing to be ignored any longer! [*Another bright flash:* BOB *has taken another self-portrait.*]
JEAN	I thought maybe veal tonight. After all that seafood. I've got some *scallopine* that must be seen to be believed! You could read a newspaper through them!
BOB	You know I never read anything. [*He tinkers with the photographic equipment.* CARLA *moves to him.*]

CARLA   You have hundreds of pictures of Bet and Larry,
         scattered all over! An entire wall montage of Jean, in the
         basement! I've seen dozens of young –
 JEAN   Peter.
CARLA   – and he hasn't been around long enough for you to
         even remember his name! But, in three whole days, you
         haven't given one thought – have you?! – to shooting me
         or my daughter?
         [BOB *chuckles, grins at* JEAN.]
CARLA   Photographing us, I mean! It's not because we're from
         the United States! You made your reputation shooting
         Americans!
 JEAN   Just like Pancho Villa! Shall we have a little more music?
CARLA   I wouldn't want you to think –!
 JEAN   We could start another Puccini! Do you know *Turandot*?
CARLA   Not now, Jean! 'Know your moment.'
  BOB   Ah! Georgie Jessel!
CARLA   [*To* BOB.] I wouldn't want you to imagine that's the only
         reason we came here! To have ourselves immortalized
         by the great Robert Rennie! We were dying to meet
         Larry's family! But I do happen to know – Jean told me
         – it's your habit to photograph visitors indiscriminately!
  BOB   It's not my habit to do anything indiscriminately!
         [*Another flash: another self-portrait.*]
         Jean should have told you that.
 JEAN   Stop baiting her!
CARLA   Exactly! That's exactly what he's been doing! From the
         moment I arrived! Baiting: ragging, tormenting –
  BOB   I know what the word means!
CARLA   Oh yes! And how to play the sport! Extremely well! You
         and Sister Bet!
  BOB   [*To* JEAN.] You know, I'm not getting a hell of lot done
         here.
 JEAN   Carla –
CARLA   Stop it, Jean! Stop protecting him! [*To* BOB.] Can't you
         show a little concern for humanity, once in your life?
         For flesh and blood, instead of that stupid toy?
  BOB   This, dear heart, is my Hasselblad 2000 –
CARLA   I don't care if it's a goddamned laser gun!
  BOB   In a way, it is.

CARLA	Why don't you just admit that you disliked and distrusted me and Linda, right from the start?!
BOB	No. Not Linda. Not from the start.
CARLA	You've gone out of your way to show us –
BOB	I never go out of my way!
CARLA	– you think Larry made a disastrous choice!
BOB	I expect Larry to make disastrous choices!
JEAN	Please –!
	[*Another flash: another self-portrait.*]
CARLA	[*To* BOB.] I wonder if it would interest you to know what percentage of his investment in video studios and video people and video toys your brother received directly from me?!
BOB	No, it would not.
CARLA	Eighty-seven!
BOB	[*To* JEAN.] Where is Larry?
CARLA	Go on, ask him if you don't believe me! It was mostly my idea, not to say investment! Larry needed focus. That's all Larry ever really needs. Eighty-seven per cent. Courtesy of my first husband. Linda's father.
BOB	Where is your first husband?
CARLA	He's dead.
BOB	He would be. Where is your second?
JEAN	He and Bet went for a walk.
BOB	Send young – Peter to fetch him!
JEAN	No.
BOB	Why isn't anyone doing as I ask?! People usually do as I ask!
JEAN	Why don't you take Carla's picture?!
CARLA	Oh no! He's not taking any pictures of me! I wouldn't allow him to!
BOB	You see?
CARLA	Not now! Not out of – pity.
BOB	Exactly! And what other reason could I possibly have?
CARLA	Son of a bitch.
BOB	Jean –?!
JEAN	I agree with her.
CARLA	Merciless old-world son of a bitch!!
BOB	Will you at least – both of you – as a special favour – sit down – let me just – use the space?!

Martha Henry (CARLA), Booth Savage (JEAN) and William Hutt (BOB).

CARLA   No!

BOB   Stand then – and be damned! Pace, prowl or pirouette! Spin like a bloody Catherine wheel, if it makes you happy!
[*Another flash: another self-portrait.*]

CARLA   Sit down, Jean. [*She sits.*] Why shouldn't he have to come up with a straight answer? Once in his life? I don't care how many times he's been on *Good Morning, America* – I want to know what I'm being – ostracized – punished for!
[*Another flash, self-portrait.... BOB looks at JEAN, then at CARLA, and sighs. He moves away from his photographic equipment, to CARLA.*]

BOB   Very well, dear heart. Let me be perfectly candid. You bore the everlasting shit out of me.

And yes, I felt that, right from the start! You want to know why?

CARLA   I merely wanted to know –

BOB   Jean was right! I will photograph almost anyone. Anything! I have but one requisite. I refuse to commit to film anything which patently lacks a soul – a spirit, an inner fire! I've gone irrevocably on record as believing that – without the fire – there is simply nothing to photograph! My laser shoots right thorugh any *corpus* uninhabited by *animus*! I would end up with a picture of the wall behind you! The empty chair in which you imagine yourself to be sitting! – Perhaps a faint residue of Helena Rubinstein, hovering near centre-of-frame!

JEAN   Bob! We are all going to regret –!

[CARLA *stops him with a gesture.* BOB *fusses with his photographic equipment, continues to* CARLA.]

BOB   The instant you set foot in this house, three days ago, you were hungry – itching to be shot! Captured! Photo-copied! You have not been a human being, dear heart, a thing of flesh and blood, not for the past three days! You've been an aching relentless series of – postures – attitudes! You knew you were coming to see the photographer, so you turned yourself into a photograph! You stalked into my world – talk about making an entrance! – like Miss Joan Crawford!! 'Look at this shot – catch this angle – snap this profile – don't miss the light along this cheekbone!' I was – how shall I say? – aghast!! Jean was aghast too. I remember it perfectly. Even young – Whoozits was aghast!

CARLA   Jean –?

JEAN   I remember it perfectly. I was intrigued.

BOB   You were –? You were not! You were aghast!

JEAN   And intrigued.

[*BOB frowns, turns back to* CARLA.]

BOB   What your avid-for-celluloid soul doesn't seem to comprehend, dear heart, is that the camera – a very sensitive beast indeed – is paralyzed by your lust! Salivating for an exposure! Don't you see? I dare not – force it to shoot you! I'd run the risk of – turning my poor old Hasselblad 2000 so permanently off – it might

never function for me again! And there I'd be, without
my – livelihood, a staff in my old age! Likewise poor old
Jean, eh? We might be forced to – to plunge into the
gaseous cauldron of rock video! God knows what!! That
is why I cannot – may not, must not! – turn my
consecrated lens upon your sinuous prefabricated
charms – dear heart! I am so hideously afraid it might
spark a mutiny amongst my – equipment!
[*Pause.*]
[CARLA *stands and moves with great dignity toward the
exit. Then she stops, turns back.*]

CARLA   It's not my problem. I don't have a problem. You have a
problem! The problem is, there's only one little piece of
you, Mister Rennie – only one organ in the proper
working order anymore! This one!! [*She taps the
camera.*]

BOB   Careful!

CARLA   This! – is the jaundiced eye which you train
on everything and everybody! I'm proud, as a matter of
fact, proud that you don't find me appealing! I turn you
off? You and your evil little eye?! I would only worry if
you wanted to take my picture! I'd be afraid I might
come out, looking as lifeless as your other old-fashioned
character studies! Your record of the new world?! Don't
make me laugh! What could you possibly know –
possibly understand – about this world – my world?! Oh
no, it's not my itch that irritates you, Brother Bob! Just
the opposite! I'm simply not dead enough to suit your
tired old – diseased old – pretentious old – solitary old –
eye!!

BOB   Oh, but you are, you absolutely are! [*He hurries to a
camera.*] Hold still and watch the birdy, Miss Crawford?
Say 'Cheese'!!

CARLA   Piss –!
[*A particularly brilliant flash:* BOB *has taken* CARLA*'s
picture.*]
– off!!

BOB   Perfect.
[*He steps back from the camera.* CARLA *swivels, gives* JEAN
an anguished look, then turns back and abruptly takes a

swipe at the camera. It topples. BOB *rushes to save it, as*
CARLA *turns, and stalks out.*]
[*Pause.*]

BOB How oddly overwrought some Yanks can be. [*He*
inspects the camera for damage.] Especially the women.
I could never live down there – bugger the advantages of
climate and economy!
[*He fusses with various photographic equipment.* JEAN
watches him.]
That is no woman of the new world! Not of the
unpolished, unfettered, unfettering world which I came
here to find. Which I found! Oh no! I absolutely reject
any suggestion that it is Mister Whitman's raw,
explosive – God! – who stares back at me with those –
shiny velvet-button eyes! It's bleeding Joan Crawford!!

JEAN And what world do you think bleeding Joan Crawford
came from?

BOB Hollywood!
[*Another flash: he has taken another self-portrait.*]
Southern California is not the new world, *copain*. It's a
cemetery – under an avocado farm – under a parking
lot!

JEAN Don't you feel maybe you overreacted?

BOB You mean to –?

JEAN Carla!

BOB Did it strike you that way?

JEAN It struck me that you attacked a dandelion with a steam
shovel.

BOB A dandelion! [*He laughs.*] Perfect!

JEAN – Do you want a drink?

BOB No. And I'm not sure that you should have one either.
[JEAN *fixes himself a drink.*]
Larry tells me that you and – his wife are – what was
Bet's phrase? – having it off.

JEAN Yes, that sounds like Bet.

BOB I almost laughed in his face! Bet actually did laugh. In
fact, she tried to persuade Larry that you and I –
[CARLA *comes back in suddenly.*]

CARLA I'm – Should you – I am in my room, our room, Larry's
and – If anyone should ask!

[*She goes out.* BOB *laughs.*]

BOB   For God's sake!

JEAN   Carla –?

BOB   I expect she expects you to follow her.

JEAN   Yes. I expect.

BOB   Well, it's your own fault! You've been drifting in her sinuous polyester wake ever since they got here.

JEAN   Ah! You noticed? Is that why you were baiting our American cousin all evening? Because I was being too attentive?

BOB   For God's sake – why should I care?

JEAN   Exactly what I was about to ask.

BOB   It was with extreme difficulty I refrained from informing poor old Lare – just how many polyester ladies there have been – over the years – in whose wakes you have drifted!

[JEAN *looks up at him, smiles.*]

'And not only women, Larry! No! My devoted domestic has drifted – over the years – with equally enthusiastic disinterest – in the wake of occasional male passers-by! Stout and lean – blond and dark – young and –thingummy!'

JEAN   [*Laughs.*] I didn't know you were keeping a chronicle! Exactly how many 'wakes' have I 'drifted in'? Over the years? My ego needs a boost – didn't you do a grand total?

BOB   Maybe.

JEAN   'Maybe.' And would that include all our little adventures – yours and mine, remember? – over the years?

BOB   Maybe. Those wouldn't add greatly to the grand total. Would they now?

JEAN   Don't you think so? And whose choice was that?

BOB   Whose –? Are you suggesting that it was mine? Mine alone?!

[JEAN *just smiles.*]

God – Jesus! I guess we haven't really known each other quite as well – in any but the occasional Biblical sense – and not that thrillingly often! – no, not quite as well as these Munchkins might like to imagine! In some ways, we've been – effectively – strangers. Efficiently! Haven't we?

JEAN 'Maybe.' [*Laughs.*] Which of your movies is this scene from, Miss Crawford?

BOB ... Actually I – think I will have a teensy-weensy nip of something! [*He fixes himself a drink.*]

JEAN You're scared. You're really scared lately. Aren't you?

BOB Never! Don't be stupid. Almost never.
[LINDA, *not yet seen, is heard calling.*]

LINDA Bet? Hello ...?!

BOB Oh, for God's bloody sake!

LINDA Bet ...?

JEAN I should see about supper. [*He starts out.*]

BOB Don't leave this room yet! I'm warning you. Do. Not.
[LINDA *comes in, cautiously carrying the blue glass sphere, which she has reassembled and glued together somehow.*]

LINDA Hi. Didn't I hear Bet's voice, just now?

BOB No!

JEAN She's gone for a walk.

LINDA Another one? With who?

JEAN Larry.

LINDA Oh. Poor Bet! – Behold! Miraculously restored by the great god Epoxy!

JEAN Good as new!

LINDA God, I hope so! [*To* BOB.] Were you photographing somebody?

JEAN Yes. His favourite model!

LINDA Really? Who's that?

BOB [*To* JEAN.] *Mange de la merde.*

LINDA Oh. [*She carefully deposits the reassembled sphere on a table at one side.*] I've been afraid you'd want to take my picture. I hate photographs! Of me, I mean. I've been known to actually break out in hives, if I have to look at pictures of myself.

BOB What a shame more people don't share your allergy! [*He adds liquor to his glass.*]For God's sake! – I just remembered! I have to be in L.A. tomorrow! Isn't it tomorrow we have to be in Los Angeles?

JEAN No.

[BET *comes in, exhausted.*]

BET   J.M. Whistler was right! Sunsets are pornographic! Especially on the water! [*She fixes herself a drink.*] That moment – when the magenta cloud droops, like a floozy's flashy knickers – and wiggles over the pink wave! Enough to make the vultures queasy! Larry's gone to his room, to swallow his customary gallon of Maalox! [*She notices the reassembled sphere.*] Hello! We found another one?

LINDA   We'd never find another one! Not half as big. I resurrected the first! What do you think?

[BET *points.*]

BET   Where's this bit?

LINDA   It must've disintegrated. I looked everywhere! Peter even loaned me a magnifying lens.

BOB   [*To* JEAN.] No, no! I'm virtually certain it is! Los Angeles! First thing tomorrow! Somebody terribly conspicuous to photograph.

[PETER *has come in.*]

BET   Baby Peter! Come see. Young America has mended our fantasy!

[PETER *inspects the sphere.*]

PETER   Shazzam!

LINDA   I resurrected it!

PETER   Well yeah, but – it doesn't look especially happy, does it?

[BET *laughs.*]

It reminds me of this photo they ran last week, in the *Province*. This guy in Chicago tried to blow himself up, wearing a – a sort of girdle of dynamite! Protesting something, I guess. Anyway, they collected him and pasted the pieces back together. He was alive – well, quasi-alive. But he didn't look very happy about it! [*He laughs.*]

JEAN   I remember the photo. – Anybody else want a drink?

PETER   Maybe I'll have a beer?

[JEAN *gives him the beer, then fixes another drink for himself.* BET *turns away from the sphere, starts out.*]

LINDA   Where are you going now?

BET   To have a nice quick shower – so I'm clean enough for a

144

nice long bath! There are only two things I cannot bear about beaches – the sand and the water! [*She is gone.*]

PETER   I should probably get cleaned up too. I'm starting to look like Doctor Frankenstein's apprentice! Crazy Fritz! [*Walking like Fritz, and taking his beer along, he starts out. As he passes* LINDA.] You look terrific!

LINDA   You negative little prick!
[*He stops in his tracks.*]

PETER   – Me?

LINDA   So what would you have done with it?! It was as much your fault as mine! Sure, just toss it out with the garbage, forget the whole thing! You have any idea how long it takes, guessing where each little microscopic piece fits? Holding it in place for a minimum of three minutes?! You don't understand anything! You didn't see her face when she found it! When it found her!

PETER   – I think maybe you inhaled too much epoxy!

LINDA   Oh sure, make some smart-ass joke! Anything at all, as long as you don't have to get involved!!

PETER   As long as I don't –?! [*He gives* BOB *and* JEAN *a brief embarrassed look, then turns back to* LINDA.] I don't even know what you're talking about!

LINDA   Bet! When she found that thing, it was like – like somebody had sent her a gift! For the first time in her life! Like there was something – out there! – that didn't have it in for her! It came from the sea! But it wasn't a filthy black mouthful, a giant wave! It was – a gift!!
[PETER *starts to speak. She doesn't give him the chance.*]
And Bet needs to feel – all of that! – a hell of a lot more than the rest of us! She deserves it a hell of a lot more!

PETER   Who says?!

LINDA   'Who says?!' Classic!
[PETER *starts out again.*]
Go on, wash your hands! Scrub off any slight urge you might have to concern yourself, with anybody or anything! You're all so damned cool and white and pure – it makes me absolutely sick!!

PETER   All I said was –!

LINDA   That is so like all of you goddamned people!
[*She starts out.* PETER *stops her.*]

145

PETER	Just a minute!! All of what goddamned people?!
LINDA	Goddamned – superior – chilly-willy Canadians!
	[BOB *and* JEAN *laugh.*]
PETER	Oh – get lost!!
LINDA	Classic!
	[PETER *starts out. She stops him.*]
LINDA	You know what Bet always says?
PETER	I truly don't give a shit!
LINDA	Classic! Typical! Bet always says, 'The principal Canadian export is the shrug!'
PETER	How bloody profound!
LINDA	You see?! Classic! You can't even react passionately – to your own incapacity for passion!
PETER	My – what?! What is all this shit?! Instant cultural analysis! Is that what Young America is majoring in this year?!
LINDA	Who says I'm majoring in anything?!
PETER	Bloody right!! Why should you?! You've got all your attitudes – ready to wear! – from Venerable Bet! Sibyl of the Permanent Sneer!!
	[BOB *laughs.* LINDA *glares at him, then moves quite close to* PETER.]
LINDA	Listen! Don't you say one more damned cool superior syllable, not about her! At least she's got some justification! If she's angry! If she's afraid! She's not just one more above-it-all Canadian wimp!!
PETER	Oh, why don't you – go – glue another fractured globe together?! Henrietta Kissinger?!
LINDA	Why don't you just – hump a polar bear?! Sergeant Preston of the Yukon?!!
	[BOB *laughs, moves to his photographic equipment.*]
PETER	[*To* LINDA.] Sergeant Preston?! Tinseltown's mincing Mountie?! Is poor old Sergeant Preston the only silly-ass Canadian stereotype you can dredge up?!
JEAN	Try Anne Murray.
BOB	*Tabar*-bloody-*nac*!!
	[*A stunningly bright flash of light:* BOB *has taken* LINDA*'s picture.*]
PETER	Christ!
LINDA	[*At the same time.*] What was that?!

BOB	*In*-bloody-*croyable*!
	[*Two more brilliant bursts of light: two more shots of* LINDA.]
JEAN	Bob!
BOB	[*At the same time.*] Perfect!
LINDA	[*At the same time.*] Damn it – was that me?!
	[*Two more flashes.* PETER *understands what's happening, and crows with laughter.*]
PETER	Shazzam! Stalking the Ugly American!!
JEAN	Stop it!
LINDA	[*To* BOB.] *Damn you –!*
BOB	[*To* JEAN.] She said she was dying to be photographed!
LINDA	You know that's not what I said!
BOB	No? Ah, I must be thinking of your – whatzits –?
PETER	Mommie Dearest!
	[*More laughter.*]
LINDA	Bob, you can't keep those pictures!
BOB	God, I get so confused! All these Yanks look alike!
LINDA	I said, you can't have them! I don't care if it's your house – that's a flagrant invasion of privacy!
BOB	The New Guineans are restless tonight! [*He grins at* JEAN.]
LINDA	I'm serious! I don't want you to even consider developing that piece of film!
PETER	As Miss America said to Bob Guccione!
	[*He and* BOB *cackle.*]
JEAN	[*At the same time.*] Stop it, Peter!
LINDA	[*At the same time.*] Shove it, Sergeant Preston!! Bob –? Listen to me!
JEAN	[*To* PETER.] You're enjoying yourself far too much!
LINDA	Bob –?
PETER	[*To* JEAN.] Jesus – you're right!
LINDA	Bob!
PETER	What's happening to me today?!
LINDA	Mister Rennie ...?!
PETER	Shit! It'd take – Aeschylus at least – to do justice to this family!! [*He rushes from the room.*]
JEAN	Better yet, Aristophanes!
LINDA	[*To* BOB.] Look at me! I'm serious!!
BOB	Have you ever noticed, Jean? Yanks always get so

	damned serious, when they discuss anything completely inconsequential.
LINDA	I am serious about those photos! I told you I hate them!
BOB	Mm. Just like your quivering mother.
LINDA	Did you take her picture?
BOB	I did.
LINDA	And I guess that made her happy?
BOB	Ecstatic!
JEAN	He's lying, Linda.
LINDA	It doesn't matter! I'm not my mother. I'm a completely different person!
BOB	I trust you have the documents to prove that?
LINDA	You know – I used to date a guy from Sausalito. He gave up photography after two years in analysis. When he realized his camera was just a phallic substitute!
BOB	Astounding! Did he also realize that any woman who obsessively collects sea shells is symbolically searching for her vagina?
JEAN	Bob, for God's sake –!
BOB	Oh no, you don't! That's my line.
	[LINDA *tries to grab the camera he used to take her picture.*]
BOB	For God's sake! [*He snatches the camera, conceals it behind his back.*]
LINDA	–What in Christ is it with you tonight?! This morning on the beach you were – I almost liked you! You weren't like most of the people I know – people your age, I mean!
BOB	Thanks, I guess.
LINDA	I'm serious!
	[BOB *chuckles. After a moment, she does too.*]
LINDA	Really. I never heard anybody say it – just say all that – flat out. About the West and the new world. Whitman. God in our faces, and in our eyes! And then, I felt I could see some – family resemblance. For the first time since we got here. Not Larry! I don't mean Larry. I could see a lot of Bet in you. A lot of you in Bet.
BOB	Betsy detests the new world.
LINDA	No, she doesn't! I know that's what she says. But you have to see – you have to hear what she really means,

beneath what she says. Don't you? And that's what I
thought I saw in you – this morning on the beach.
Stripped right down to your convictions – your squint
and your grin – I liked you! Whatever else you were
wearing – your reputation, your age – who cares?! I
didn't notice that stuff! – So what happened to you
anyway? Since this morning?
[*Pause.*]
[BOB *suddenly flips the magazine of the camera open,
rips out the entire roll of film in one long strip, and
extends it slowly to* LINDA.]

BOB   Take it. Go on. You're right. I'm serious: take
it!
[LINDA *smiles, takes the roll of film.*]

LINDA   I think maybe I'll go – check out China Beach – by
moonlight. If anybody asks, that's where I am, okay?
[*She starts out, then turns back, gives* BOB *a quick kiss.*] It
ought to be magic! A full moon! Well, quasi-full!
[*She laughs and goes out, taking the ruined roll of film
with her.* BOB *smiles, then moves to fix himself another
drink.* JEAN *stares out the window.*]

BOB   You know, that's a – a rather intriguing girl, after all! I
think I'm in love! [*He laughs.*] I feel terrific! I think I feel
terrific. How do you feel?

JEAN   Like going over to Vancouver. First thing tomorrow.

BOB   Vancouver? Do we have to go to Vancouver?

JEAN   I have to go.

BOB   You? Whatever for?

JEAN   Because I have to get out of here! Away from all this.
Right away.
[*Pause.*]

BOB   You mean that you're – taking a little holiday? With pay,
of course?

JEAN   No. That's not what I mean.
[*Pause.*]

BOB   Ah. – For God's sake!

JEAN   God can look after himself nowadays! He prefers it that
way – don't you?

BOB   So this is what's been on your mind lately?

JEAN   Much longer than lately.

[BOB *fusses briefly, distractedly with his photographic equipment.*]

BOB   *Eh bien – alors –* I can't help feeling – once Larry and his unruly herd have been driven back to 'the old south pasture' – in a week or two – (maybe you should go skiing, God, it's been a long time!) – it will inevitably occur to you – there's simply nowhere else for you to be – to go – to stay – What are you thinking? Right now?

JEAN   I've always regretted you're not an opera buff.

BOB   Jesus God! Have I gone mad? What's-his-name was right! This is all too much like old misery-guts Aeschylus at his worst – best – whatever!

JEAN   No – I just think our lives might've been much simpler. If I could quote something from *Rosenkavalier* – something you'd recognize and understand, right away! Or from *Manon.* Instead of having to rely on just the words. Words mean too little in English. Too much inflection, too little sense. '*Il le faut, il le faut, et c'est là l'histoire –*'

BOB   Are you trying to say it would be easier for you – to shit on my entire world now – if you could sing a little song while doing so?!

JEAN   Something like that. With English horn *obbligato*!

BOB   I loathe opera! Anyone with a twinge of taste loathes opera! – All right, for God's sake! I'm sorry! Sorry I attacked your *Dandelion of the Golden West* with a steam thing – hammer – whatever! So I'll apologize, goddamn you, I'll apologize to her!

JEAN   This has got bugger-all to do with Carla! – Believe me, Bob! It's to do with me! Just me.

BOB   And me also – just a tad – wouldn't you say? The most agonizing three days of my entire endless life! And you run out on me?! Because I'm a little – testy?!
[JEAN *laughs, turns back, stares out the window again.*]
Twelve – thirteen years! Isn't it? Thereabouts?

JEAN   Closer to fifteen.

BOB   Fifteen bleeding years! Look at the lad! How easy for him, to tidy all that away! – Remember that night we were stranded in Saskatchewan – sat up and laughed

ourselves into oblivion, over a shoplifted bottle of
Scotch?

[JEAN *laughs but doesn't look at him.*]

And, dear God, if I actually enumerated each and every
night – that I have lain awake – listening to you snore in
the next room –!

JEAN I don't snore.

BOB Listening to your silence then! Or – in the good ol'
cockroach-and-smoked-meat sandwich days –
Montreal, remember? – listening to you thrash about on
that sway-backed leopard-skin plastic sofa! – I have lain
awake – planning what both of us were to accomplish
the next day – playing both our roles, in effect – fulfilling
both our ambitions, dreaming both our dreams! And
happy to do it! Goddamning my fatherland, motherland,
along with, inevitably, those bloody money-grubbing,
opportunity-snatching bloody Yanks! All the while,
singing the praises of this! – great all-embracing, all-
nurturing dominion! Where I discovered – we
discovered –! We might finally have discovered –!! [*He
moves to fix himself another drink, watching* JEAN
continuously.]

BOB Well – what did blundering, half-blind old Bobby
expect? That there was enough old world in you to
understand the concept of loyalty? Enough new world
that you would always speak your mind? Enough
Quebec that – if you were going to bugger off and bugger
up my entire life – you at least wouldn't bugger off
without giving me a chance to – negotiate?!

[*He laughs. So does* JEAN, *more quietly.*]

No – no – no – More than that. More than all of that!
Affection! Yes, Christ, why shouldn't I call it love, if I
want to?! Not romantic, not physical maybe – not often
physical – but real, yes! Honest, yes! More than a job!
More than work for wages!

JEAN It was more! You know it was.

BOB I thought you were my friend!! I thought the work – my
work! – was important to you! – And beyond all that –
beyond virtually everything – I thought – we were –
somehow – magically – alike! Attracted! Bonded!

Epoxied! Isn't that a scream? Jesus God -- old Bobby!
Enough to drive you mad! Foundering old one-eyed
crypto-British pompous feeble-hearted proto-neurotic
greedy pontifical shambling old – snap-shooter!
Shotsnapper!! – Which is it?! [*He is in tears.*]

BOB What are you thinking? Right now!
[JEAN *looks at him.*]

JEAN That it's definitely Aristophanes! Classic farce! The
egocentric old scoundrel dissolves – in what might
almost pass for tears!

BOB Egocentric? I?!
[JEAN *turns away.*]

JEAN Ay-ay-ay-ay-ay –!

BOB Come here! You! Come over here and look me straight in
the eye!

JEAN This is a family obsession!
[BOB *moves to him.*]

BOB Straight in this – now red – and liquid – but perfectly
focused eye! Look at me! Stop shaking!

JEAN I'm not shaking!

BOB Now – just say it! Say 'Fifteen years.' Just say that.

JEAN Fifteen years.

BOB As if you meant it!! As if you were reflecting upon –
refracting! – fifteen years!! Thousands of weeks –
hundreds of thousands of days! Our mutual giggles and
gaffes – missed planes, missed boats – difficult
moments, unbearable hours – [*He slumps onto the sofa.*]
– for my sake – I know, all for my sake! And my work!
And now – dare to say to me – fifteen years! Say – it –
[JEAN *slowly sits beside him, touches is hand, gives him a
short, but not light, kiss.*]

JEAN Fifteen years.
[*At the same time, a blinding flash of light:* BOB *has taken
a photograph of them together.*]

BOB Perfect.
[JEAN *stands immediately, stalks away. At the same time,*
LARRY *comes in, utterly distraught.*]

LARRY What in bloody hell is going on around here?!

BOB Jean is pissed and talking wild! Help me sober him up.

LARRY No, no, no! I want to know who is responsible!

JEAN	That's not a good question tonight.
BOB	Or in this century!
LARRY	Carla was – whizzing around the bedroom – throwing things – practically climbing the walls! I've never seen her like that! I had to hold her down on the bed! Tears streaming down her cheeks! Her chin was wobbling! She looked at me – like I'm a complete stranger – and she made a – a squeaking noise! Like one of those little rubber animals with a whistle in the back of its head! I'm scared! Even when we nearly went bankrupt, couple of months back, she only broke a couple of snifters, and set the neighbors' hedge on fire!
JEAN	She's not setting anything here on fire? [*He starts out.*]
LARRY	Who the hell cares?! [*He stops* JEAN.] I want to know how she got that way! What did you do to her?!
	[JEAN *looks at* BOB.]
	[*To* BOB.] What did you do to her?!
BOB	To – whom?
LARRY	My wife!
BOB	You mean – Joan?
LARRY	Carla!!
BOB	It wasn't me! It was – Puccini.
	[*He topples over, slowly, on the sofa.* BET *comes in, her hair up in a towel.*]
BET	'Good morning, everyone!' I'm human again!
BOB	Again? [*He laughs.*]
BET	Larry? What've you done to him?
	[*She fixes herself a drink.* JEAN *goes out, unnoticed.*]
LARRY	My wife has just fallen completely apart!
BET	Well, speak to your stepdaughter. She's the miracle worker! [*She points to the reassembled sphere.*]
LARRY	Goddamnit, I'm serious! She hasn't been herself since lunch today! These sadistic bastards did or said something –! [*He notices that* JEAN *has left.*] All right, where did he go?! Where is that – amphibious son of a bitch?!
BOB	'Larry, Larry, Huge and hairy, Ladies find him frightful scary!' Remember that?

LARRY	Good God! He's gone to Carla's – to our room!
BET	It's my fervent prayer he's gone to start supper!
BOB	I never liked that east room!
BET	I could eat a migrating whale!
LARRY	Don't you realize?! He's gone to my wife!!
BET	He's gone to the kitchen, Lare!
BOB	He's gone to Vancouver.
LARRY	[*and* BET] Vancouver?
BOB	He'll be back, don't worry. I'm not worried!
LARRY	What's going on? Did you send him to Vancouver, so as to avoid any more trouble?
BOB	Trouble? Have we got trouble?
BET	'Have we got rats?' asked the Mayor of Hamelin.
LARRY	Shut up, Betsy! [*To* BOB.] Haven't you caught on yet? What's wrong with you? Haven't you got eyes?!
BOB	What a tactless question! – I've got one!
LARRY	You should be in bed!
BOB	I should be in Los Angeles! The cemetery, not the avocado thingummy!
LARRY	This is insane! My wife is down there – sobbing her heart out to that – French – meringue-maker! I'm telling you, she is – beside herself! A squeaking emotional disaster area!!
	[CARLA *comes in, calm, wearing her glasses, eating a Greek pastry.*]
CARLA	Hi.
LARRY	– Thank God! [*He hurries to her.*] Baby Duck? Are you all right?!
CARLA	Did you see the sunset, sweetheart? Miraculous! Like something out of – What was that movie with Charlton Heston?
BET	*Planet of the Apes?*
LARRY	Bet –!
CARLA	I've never seen anything so spectacular! What an amazing country! How lucky you are, Bob.
BOB	Mm?
LARRY	Darling? Are you okay? You want to go back to the room? You want to talk?

CARLA   And the mighty Pacific! Like one big envelope of glass –
        which somebody was slipping the sun into!
LARRY   I'm telling you – I was scared! Some vital organ was
        threatening to seize up!
        [CARLA *gives him a quick kiss, then moves away.*]
CARLA   I mean – this country!! Not just this house, or China
        Beach, or the Island! This country!! It struck me, the
        moment we drove across the border! I said to Linda, 'Do
        you feel that? A change in the air? Two hundred years
        of American custom and confusion just evaporated,
        angel – like the morning fog!' Didn't I say that, Larry?
        And I meant it!
        [*They watch her. She eats and talks.*]
        God, I think it's remarkable! Look out that window – go
        on!
        [LARRY *moves to look out the window.*]
        You can just make out the lighthouse, at Pillar Point.
        Washington state! We're that close. They could hang
        glide to us from over there! But it's not the same
        country! Not the same at all! Suddenly I understand
        why you chose this place, Bob! Up here you must feel so
        – weightless – careless – guiltless! God, it makes you
        light-headed! – When I went for my swim this morning,
        the water was so cold, and smelled so fresh, so unused!
        I never smelled anything like that in California. Or even
        Colorado! I thought, 'That's Canada! This is not the
        same tired old water that's washing up over there, on
        Pillar Point!' And I just wanted – to remind all of you –
        it's not like that everywhere! So – enjoy your freedom –!
        [*She gives* LARRY *another quick kiss.*] – your lack of
        history! [*She gives* BOB *a brief pat or kiss.*] Be and do and
        – behave however you please! [*She gives* BET *a short
        smile.*] Openly! Without guilt! – There. End of party
        piece!
        [*She finishes the pastry, licks her fingers.* BOB *suddenly
        bursts into song.*]
BOB   'Yankee Doodle went to London!
        Riding on a pony –!'
LARRY   Bob!
BOB   'Stuck a feather in his bum –!'

LARRY	Bobby!!
BOB	'And called it macaroni!'
CARLA	Well – nighty-night! [*She goes out.*]
LARRY	Sweetheart –?!
	[BOB *continues his song. Now* BET *joins in.*]
BET	[*and* BOB]
	'Yankee Doodle, keep it up!
	Yankee Doodle Dandy!
	Mind the music and the step,
	And with the girls –!'
	[LARRY *turns on them.*]
LARRY	You – damned – gutless – rotten – limey – swine!!
BOB	Aaaaww!
LARRY	Good God! Have you no understanding –?!
BOB	Betty-petti'?
LARRY	– no bloody compassion at all?!
BOB	Is Laresy testy?
LARRY	If not for my wife –?!
BET	Laresy's testy!
LARRY	– at least for me?!
BOB	'Larry, Larry,
	Huge and hairy,
	Ladies find him –!'
LARRY	I'm truly disappointed! In you especially, Bet! Bob's the nearest thing to a genius! Not to mention totally sloshed!
BOB	Hear, hear!
LARRY	But I'm seriously appalled – disgusted by –!
	[PETER *has come in, wearing a small red rubber ball on the end of his nose, like a clown.* LARRY *sees him, jumps.*]
PETER	What's wrong with Carla?
LARRY	Nothing!
PETER	I passed her in the hall. She was white as a sheet.
LARRY	What do you want?! She didn't get much sun! She's been inside all day with the – Puccini! [*He calls softly down the corridor.*] Baby ...?!
	[PETER *looks at* BOB, *who has closed his eyes, and slumped even further down into the sofa.*]
PETER	Jesus! He looks dead.
BET	Well, he didn't get much sun either.

PETER	Has anybody seen Linda?
BET	No. Are you supposed to be Ronald McDonald? [PETER *shakes his head 'No.'*]
PETER	Emmett Kelly! You know – 'Weary Willie'? [*He acts like 'Willie.'*]
BET	So it's no use asking you for a cheeseburger?
LARRY	Maybe she's just gone to bed. You think maybe she's gone to bed?
PETER	Linda?
LARRY	No! Linda's mother! My wife!!
PETER	Maybe. [*To* BET.] Whenever I feel like unwrapping the old single-edge razor blades, it always helps if I make myself look silly. Ever try it?
BET	Naturally! You think I've always looked like this?! [PETER *laughs. A low rumbling noise commences, beneath the room.*]
LARRY	Listen! What's that?!
PETER	Somebody's leaving us?
LARRY	That's not the ocean?! [*He moves to the window, looks out.*] Sounds like a bloody tidal wave!
BET	It wouldn't dare – when I'm not looking!
PETER	It's the automatic door. The garage! We're right on top of it. [LARRY *looks at him.*]
LARRY	The – garage?!
PETER	Sounds like your car. [LARRY *turns back to the window. Car headlights flash across his face. He points.*]
LARRY	Holy shit! That's – my car!!
BET	Aha.
LARRY	Listen to me, dammit! That's the car! Somebody's stealing my car!
BET	Is it actually yours, Lare? Or Carla's?
LARRY	What difference does that make?! Good God! You – bunch of – vegetables! We could all be robbed and murdered, and you sit here –! [JEAN *has come in with a tray of* hors d'oeuvre. *He extends it to* LARRY.]
JEAN	Hungry?
LARRY	Leave me alone! Somebody's stealing my bloody car!

JEAN	It's Carla.
LARRY	It's –?! You're full of shit!!
	[*He rushes out.* JEAN *offers the* hors d'oeuvre.]
JEAN	Hungry?
PETER	No.
BET	I am!
	[*She and* JEAN *eat.* JEAN *glances at* BOB's *condition.*]
JEAN	Oh-oh. Was this one really singing 'Yankee Doodle'?
BET	An unreasonable fascsimile thereof.
JEAN	He used to sing it, years ago. Whenever we visited the States. He thought the Yanks would be flattered. But they weren't allowing any lousy Brit to sing 'Yank-My-Doodle, It's-A-Dandy!'
	[*He and* PETER *laugh.*]
BET	Why not? A lousy Brit wrote it. – Where's Carla going, Jean? You know, don't you?
JEAN	– Vancouver.
BET	God's truth?
JEAN	I'm meeting her there, some time tomorrow. We're – how shall I say? – eloping.
	[BET *frowns, takes more* hors d'oeuvre.]
BET	Congratulations. [*To* PETER.] If you don't make a novel out of this, you deserve to be a poet!
	[LARRY *rushes back in.*]
LARRY	It was Carla! I think it really was Carla!
BET	Better eat something, Lare. Keep your strength up!
LARRY	I don't get it! I don't get any of it! She wasn't angry! You saw her!
BET	Look at poor Bobby! Ssssh. Peter – grab a camera! Let's get a snapshot of this!
	[*They giggle.* PETER *brings* BET *a camera.* JEAN *watches them.* LARRY *paces.*]
LARRY	And I'm the crumb, I'm the goat! All day they've been on my case: 'What's wrong with Larry? Why are you acting that way, Larry?!'
	[BET *prepares, focuses the camera with* PETER's *help.*]
	My wife's gone for a midnight ramble – along the world's most perilous bloody back road! She drives like a maniac at the best of times! My big brother, the genius, is in a drooling alcoholic stupor! My big brother's

boyfriend has been chasing after my wife all day – like a toad in heat!! My anti-social stepdaughter's got a crush on my anti-social sister! But I'm the clod! I'm the asshole!!

[PETER *has removed his red rubber clown's nose and, very cautiously, clamped it onto* BOB's *nostrils.* BOB *doesn't stir.* BET *titters.*]

PETER   [*To* JEAN.] Have you seen Linda?

JEAN   She's down at the beach.

LARRY   'What on earth is wrong with you, Larry?! How can you be so bloody – desultory?!!'

[BET *takes* BOB's *picture: a brilliant flash of light. She,* PETER *and* JEAN *laugh. Suddenly the reassembled glass sphere spontaneously explodes into a thousand bright fragments. They gasp and stare.* BOB *wakes up, looks around, unruffled, still wearing the red nose.*]

BOB   Was that the end? – The actual end?

China Beach. A small driftwood fire, burnt down to embers.

    LINDA *and* PETER *are near the fire, wound round one another. They are both wearing round red clown noses. They kiss, and start to embrace more intimately.* PETER *suddenly springs away from her, grabbing his crotch.*

PETER   Ouch! What's that?!
    [*She laughs.*]

LINDA   Sorry. [*She takes something from her jeans pocket.*]

LINDA   *Granatoma excurvata*! A deep water shell, washed up in perfect condition! You know how rare that is?
    [PETER *sighs, moves near her again.*]

LINDA   Also, it's the only member of its *genus* they've discovered so far.

PETER   Uh-oh! Lots of inbreeding, eh?

LINDA   Worse yet. It's ambixesual!

PETER   Just like God or Walt Whitman?
    [*She laughs.*]

LINDA   You're sick!

PETER   I told you – I'm a poet!

LINDA Which entitles you to special treatment?

PETER Absolutely! I'm a deep-water shell, washed up in perfect condition! You know how rare –?

LINDA Shut up!

[*They embrace, kiss.*]

PETER So – What now?

LINDA Aren't we going in?

PETER Into the house?

LINDA Into the water!

PETER You know how cold it's going to be?

LINDA Isn't that how polar bears like it?

[*They laugh, kiss.*]

PETER Actually I meant – what are you going to do? Now.

LINDA Oh! – Stick around. Probably stick around for a while. If Bob'll let me. You think that's completely crazy?

PETER Maybe. I don't even know if he'll want me around. I don't know what he's going to do. It was Jean who – got him from one day to the next. I don't know if he can manage, all by himself. I'm not much use, I know that!

[*They start to kiss again.*]

LINDA Ssshh! What's that?

PETER What?

[BOB, *not yet seen, is heard, singing softly.*]

[*He comes in, carrying a voluminous sleeping bag.* PETER *and* LINDA *move apart.*]

BOB Good evening. Everyone. [*He drops the sleeping bag, then sits.*] May I borrow your fire? Go right ahead with – whatever. I'm here for the duration! Ever since I bought this place, I've been meaning to spend a night on the beach. Never got round to it. But now is a time for –

fulfilling old promises – making fresh starts!
[*Pause.*]

PETER Did you have a little sleep? Up at the house?

BOB I did. And woke to a terrifying medley of distant sounds! Not bloody distant enough. Larry sniffling and sniveling. Jean snapping his Godforsaken suitcases shut!

LINDA What about Bet?

BOB I didn't hear Bet. Bet was quiet. That's rather worrying, isn't it? – Aren't you cold? I'm cold. Your noses are frostbitten!
[*They laugh.* PETER *gets to his feet.*]

PETER We were just going for a splash! Want to come along? A little polar bear plunge?

BOB Are you demented – or just young?

PETER Water that cold is always a stimulant. Guaranteed to shock you into a fresh start!

BOB There is a world of difference between shock and stimulation, Peter. You two are ripe for the one. I'm barely strong enough for the other.
[JEAN, *not yet seen, calls.*]

JEAN Bob? Hello! Anybody?!
[PETER *calls.*]

PETER Down here!
[*He and* LINDA *remove their clown noses.* JEAN *comes in, moves down the beach to them.*]

JEAN *Salut, tout le monde.*

BOB *Ave atque vale!* Are you still hanging about?

JEAN Just going. I wanted to say goodbye.

BOB 'Bye.
[LINDA *gets to her feet.*]

LINDA We were just going too.

PETER Right!

LINDA For a quick splash.

PETER Polar bear plunge!
[*They begin removing their clothes, tossing them aside.*]

LINDA Smell the water! It only smells like that at night!

PETER The gentle fragrance of ice crystals! 'Bye, Jean. Be careful. [*He shakes* JEAN*'s hand.*]

BOB 'If you can't be good.'

JEAN	Goodbye –
BOB	Peter.
JEAN	I know! Goodbye, Peter. Linda.
LINDA	Tell Mother I'll drop her a postcard, let her know what's happening!
JEAN	She's going to phone you, from Vancouver!
LINDA	Sure! Whatever! [*She runs toward the water, still shedding clothes.*] Get the lead out, Sergeant Preston!! [*She disappears, but can be heard, laughing, gasping, splashing, off.*]
PETER	[*To* BOB.] If we're not back in ten minutes, Nanook – send the huskies!
	[*He and* BOB *laugh.* PETER *runs toward the water –*]
PETER	*Banzai,* Captain America!!
	[*– and disappears. He and* LINDA *can be heard intermittently, laughing, splashing.* BOB *turns, watches them for a moment, then turns back and begins unrolling the sleeping bag.*]
JEAN	Bob?
BOB	So long. Drive carefully, won't you?
JEAN	Carla will do most of the driving. I'll try to sell my car in Vancouver.
BOB	Oh good! Cast it all off! You always believed in traveling light! Well, tell Carla to drive carefully. You wouldn't want to end up as just one more hideous highway statistic!
JEAN	Bob – don't.
BOB	A day or two, *copain,* you'll be in southern California! Lovely. You always enjoyed parking lots – avocados –!
JEAN	I don't know about 'a day or two.' We're going to take our time. Maybe get to know one another on the way down.
BOB	Oh good! I hope so!
	[*He has difficulty unzipping the sleeping bag.* JEAN *tries to help him.*]
BOB	It's all right! I'm – all right! Let go![*He shoves* JEAN *away, finally manages to unzip the bag. He folds it open, sits on it.*] I can look after myself, for God's sake! I prefer it that way!
	[*A distant burst of laughter from* PETER *and* LINDA. BOB

looks in that direction. JEAN *moves to the opposite side of the fire, looks at* BOB.]

JEAN Times change, Bob. People change. Time changes people. When we first got together, times weren't so good – for either of us. Remember? I was still pretty young. It made perfect sense for me to work for you. To wrap up and put into storage any piece of me that didn't fit in with you! With your work! Yes? I don't regret it. – But I'm not pretty young anymore.

BOB No. Neither one, nor the other.

JEAN All right! So it's time to get the rest of me, the bits I never used, out of storage! Find out if they need – reconditioning, overhauling.

BOB And you feel – Carla is the proper mechanic to assist in your – tune-up?

JEAN Why not? She's tough.

BOB Yes, she's – that.

JEAN More than that! She's interested.

BOB For the time being.

JEAN All right, but it's enough! She's interested in every bit of me. Not just the convenient or efficient bits. For the time being. Sometimes that's all one really requires. – You can afford to buy top of the line now, whatever you need. Cook, typist, gardener, dark room assistant. You won't have to rely on somebody who's mostly – winging it.

BOB And hairy scary old Larry? I notice he's one component of this – ecstatic equation! – everyone seems to have conveniently forgot! I suppose it's going to be just peachy keen for Larry too?

JEAN Maybe. He's driving in with me.
    [*Pause.*]

BOB Pardon?

JEAN He's going over to Vancouver with me. To meet Carla.
    [*Pause.*]

BOB Pardon?

JEAN He says he just wants to see if it can't all be sorted out. To everybody's satisfaction. That's what he says.
    [*Pause.*]

BOB Pardon?
    [LARRY, *not yet seen, calls.*]

LARRY	Jean –?! *Mon ami?!*
JEAN	Down here!
	[LARRY *comes in, brushed and tidied.*]
LARRY	Aren't we ready to go? I'm ready to go! – Hiya, Bobby.
BOB	*Bon soir.*
LARRY	God, it's cold! Practically Alaska! Still, it's – bracing! Bracing can be good too! – Jean told you –?
BOB	*Oui.*
LARRY	How about this handy-dandy adaptable old Brit, eh? Got to move with the times! Isn't that what they say?
BOB	Times change. People change. Time changes people.
LARRY	Right on! God, I wish I'd said that!
BOB	I wish I hadn't.
	[*Loud shouts, war cries, splashing, etc. from* LINDA *and* PETER, *off.*]
LARRY	Who's that? My – our –?
BOB	Linda. And young Peter. Polar bears!
	[LARRY *calls off to* PETER *and* LINDA.]
LARRY	Hello?! Hello, babies!! How ya doin'?!
	[*Faint garbled replies from* LINDA *and* PETER, *off.* LARRY *calls.*]
	Bracing as bloody hell, isn't it?! You look terrific!! [*Turns to* BOB.] Are they all right? Is Linda going to be okay?
BOB	Everybody is going to be okay.
LARRY	No, I meant, how is she going to feel about –?
BOB	I know what you meant! Everybody is going to be okay.
LARRY	You're – Bobby? – you're upset with me.
BOB	Not at all! Merely aghast. No matter. I'm often aghast nowadays. On the road to becoming permanently aghast.
LARRY	Life's a stinker, eh? Things get screwed around. I'm sorry.
BOB	Don't be. Aghast is better than – anaesthetized. It keeps me young. Haggard. But young.
LARRY	I've just got to try and – hold things together. For myself! Jean understands. Your Jean is being a real brick about all this!
BOB	*Un brave type, ce garçon. D'accord.*
	[JEAN *has moved away from them, away from the fire.*]
JEAN	We should go! The first ferry leaves at dawn.

[LARRY *touches* BOB's *shoulder.*]

LARRY I'll phone from Vancouver.

BOB Or drop me a postcard. Send a smoke signal!

[LARRY *turns, calls toward* LINDA *and* PETER, *off.*]

LARRY 'Bye-bye, babies!! Take care!!

[*No audible reply from* PETER *or* LINDA. LARRY *turns back.*]

Take care, Bobby.

BOB Oh, infinite – infinite care!

[LARRY *and* JEAN *go out, talking.*]

LARRY I put my bags in the back seat. We can shift them to the trunk, after we pick up the Baby Duck. I mean, if it's feasible to share transportation? All the way home? I can't wait for you to see that kitchen! One of our whiz kids from the studio put it in – nice-looking kid. You're going to think you've died and gone to Heaven!

[*He laughs. They can no longer be seen. Voices fade.*]

You know, I was thinking – she might get a giggle out of it! How do you say 'Baby Duck'? In French?

JEAN You don't.

[*Pause.*]

BOB 'Bye. [*He sings softly.*]

Ad-dio, mia Cali-for-nia—!

[*Sounds of* PETER *and* LINDA *in the sea, very faintly now, off.* BOB *crawls into the sleeping bag, ooches nearer the embers of the fire.*]

'Bobby, Bobby,
Found a hobby,
Rode it 'til his knees were knobby!'

[BET *comes in, dressed as in the first scene, intoning.*]

BET 'Nothing of him that doth fade –
But doth suffer a sea-change –
Into something rich and strange.'

Bobsy.

BOB Betsy.

BET I was down at the cove. The large cove – or so I thought.

William Hutt (BOB) and Susan Wright (BET).

Sitting there, sphinx-like, in the grotto. Baby Peter's quasi-magic quasi-grotto – or so I thought. Waiting for the tide to come in and claim me! Waiting, along with the crab claws and dead sand-dollars. All of a sudden, I thought, 'This can't be the large cove! Peter said it's miles and miles away! And this is no grotto, quasi- or otherwise! It's just a filthy little, stinking little cave! A quasi-cave! And besides, the tide's not bloody well coming in, it's bloody well going out!!' I can't do anything right! I got the wrong cove, Bobby. Wrong time, wrong place – crikey! 'A very shallow monster. A most poor credulous monster!'

[*From the sea, a splash and cry, quite distant.* BET *looks in that direction.*]

Ferdinand and Miranda!

BOB Polar bears! Gone for a splash – before the scent of moonlight's off the wave!

BET 'A very ancient and fish-like smell.'

BOB And – Larry's off. Did you know?

BET Larry's been off for years!

BOB No, he's – decamped, I mean. With my – With Jean and *The Girl of the Golden Whatzits*. I was – I must confess – quasi-aghast. How about you?

BET Sorry. I can't even muster a 'quasi' for that jolly threesome. Those whom Hollywood hath joined together, let no man put asunder! – I am sorry.

BOB Don't be.

[*More laughter, etc., off.* BET *looks in that direction.*]

Thinking of joining them?

BET Me? [*She laughs.*] Sitting down there – in my mind's grotto – I suddenly found myself thinking about – my first, well, my only commission. Do you remember? That asthmatic old pouf from the vanity press asked me to do a few little pictures for his vellum edition of *The Tempest*. So I did a few little pictures. Which he rejected after a single mincing glance! 'No, no, my dear! Not what we had in mind at all! Not half evocative enough!' Oh, I knew what he had in mind. Young Ferdinand, stripped to the waist, a torso like the Belvedere Apollo – hauling his bloody big log about! – Not too surprisingly, I had concentrated on Master Will's feckless fools. Moon-calf Caliban. Trinculo, the jester without one good jest. Wretched – besotted Stephano!

[*Music.*]

BOB In a blue mood, Betsy?

[*She laughs, or tries to.*]

Don't be! Look at me. I'm not blue. I won't be, in a few weeks. Or days.

BET I'm tired. Bone weary of waiting! Waiting for that ship – that high tide, that special friend, that special moment, that special life – even, Christ, that special death! – to come sailing past. I'd board it, oh yes, shamelessly! I've been waiting at threshholds, eyes and ears wide open, to seize my opportunity – any opportunity! Living on stale ale and confetti so long – well, that's always been my diet, hasn't it? Bumping through life on Dad's pneumatic tyres, on Mum's feeble hopes, and my own feebler ones! And now you'll put me up in the spare room with your botched portraits and unsuccessful still lifes – and I – am – past – bearing – it!! Oh, God's truth! Ready to throw in the towel, the turpentine and smock and *chiaroscuro*! There was just one consolation for me – in your new world, Bobby! My annihilating, unstoppable, all-embracing black wave! I was convinced by a dead friend – by signs external and einternal – that the world might end here – and soon! – and I might end with it! You can't know how I looked foirward to that! No more waiting! No more lost sleep, lost waking dreams!! But – I can't believe – even in that – not anymore.

BOB   Why not?

BET   Nothing is ending here! I can see that! Nothing here is old – or sick of self – or tired of waiting!

BOB   We're old, Bet.

BET   One of us is! You're a child! You always were a baby. You'll go to your grave an infant. But I'm – of the old world, the old ways. I crawl in the traditional direction!

BOB   Change directions!

BET   Oh Christ, Bobby –!! If it were that easy –!

BOB   No! I know it's not! But I do believe it's possible! Possibility is a rich and strange local beverage! One cannot resist it forever. I'm proof of that. When I first came to this continent – just as the glaciers began their retreat! – I was skeptical too. All those pure sharp faces, flushed with God and – incontrovertible optimism! I desperately wanted to blot them out! Paint them – etch them small and ape-like, with a colossal dash of old-world sarcasm! But they resisted! They resisted everything – except accuracy – the child's eye of my camera! To capture this world – you have to relax all those frantic old muscles – and let it capture you! If it is the fresh eye, the blistered but buoyant heart that I

found here – which will send me to my grave an infant –
I'll hang onto them! I won't trade them for your
exhausted vision – your dry wit and your bloody black
wave! Finally, all those things are silence. And I – want
to sing!

[LINDA *and* PETER *are heard, not so far away
now, splashing, laughing.* BOB *looks in that
direction.*]

'O, wonder! How many goodly creatures are there here!
How beauteous –!'

BET Stop! Stop now! I haven't had a bite today – except
Jean's fish paste and biscuits! I'm already light-headed.
One more rapturous word from you, I swear I'll go into
convulsions!

BOB Change directions! You can, you absolutely can! There's
nothing for you to wait for anymore. Nothing – no one.
Now we – are waiting for you! You need us. Here and
now. And we need you!

[*She weeps. He moves to her, holds her.*]

You and I, Bet – between us, we have known age – and
shabbiness and struggle! But now – here we are. Still
alive! Unique and needed. Right place. Right time. Right
cast of characters at last! – Right?

[*Laughing and splashing in the shallows, nearby, off.*]

And here come our young sea lions! Our irresistible
polar bears! Look at them, sis!

BET I am.

[*She moves away from him, wipes her face. He crawls
back into the sleeping bag.*]

BOB Look! Open your eyes!!

[LINDA *and* PETER *run in, glistening wet, gathering up their
clothes and clutching them for warmth.*]

PETER Lord-lifting-Jesus!

LINDA That was so – great!! Am I glowing? I feel like I'm
glowing!

PETER I can't feel anything!

BOB You want me to stir up the fire again?

LINDA No –

BET You're crazy to stir things up tonight – aren't you,
Bobby?

LINDA – it won't really help! I know what! [*She moves to the sleeping bag, crawls in beside* BOB.]

LINDA Scoot over!

BOB Scoot –?

LINDA Aaaaahh! That's better! There's room enough for an army in here!

BOB I – I didn't invite any armies. Did I, Bet?

BET No, but you've had worse ideas.

PETER You know how weird you look? You two, snuggled up in your damned cocoon?! [*He laughs.*]

LINDA Does it bother you?

PETER Is it supposed to?

LINDA Don't fight it, Chilly-Willy! Join us!

PETER Join –? Are you serious?

LINDA Us Yanks are always serious! Aren't we, Bob?
[PETER *hesitates only an instant, then rushes to the sleeping bag, crawls in beside* LINDA.]

PETER Scoot over!

LINDA [*To* BOB.] Scoot over!

BOB I'm half in the fire already!

LINDA There's lot of room!

PETER This is – terrific! Christ, you're right! I must've died and gone to Heaven!
[*They laugh.*]

LINDA And there's still lots of room for wings and harps! Loads of room! Come one, come all!
[*Pause.*] [*They all sit up in the sleeping bag, and look at* BET.]

BOB Loads of room, Betsy.

LINDA Come on!

BET 'Misery acquaints a man with strange bedfellows!'

PETER What misery? Come on, for Christ's sake!

LINDA Bet? Are you all right?

BET Right as rain!

PETER Ssshh! That's not a word we use lightly. Not in British Columbia!

LINDA I'm snug as a snail!

PETER Yeah, me too. Except for my nose!
[*He extracts the round red clown nose from his clothes, puts it on.* LINDA *follows suit. They extend their hands*

toward BET, *in a gesture welcoming her into the sleeping bag. So does* BOB. BET *moves away from them.*]

BET Up there – two little lights moving through the dark! Look! Is that from the road? Or that quasi-inhabited little place – where one catches the silly little bus?

LINDA Come on in, Bet! Don't you want to?

BOB She has to! She can't resist forever.

[*The first faint grey smudge of dawn appears above the trees.*]

BET Yes, I'll – definitely check out that little bus! First thing tomorrow. I have to go!

[*She looks back at them. They are still gesturing welcome.*]

I'm just not – ready for it! I'd never 'fit in'! I don't understand this – rough magic! – this time and place! God's truth is: it's just not ready for me! – I can't, Bobby! Truly – I can't!

[*A cool luminous haze drifts up from the water, across the beach, partially obscuring the scene.*]

I know myself. I know when it's time for this – this freckled lump of the old world to pick itself up – and move on! Time to go back to the – back where I – Time to go!

[BOB *stirs the embers, which glow through the haze.* LINDA *hums or sings without words, to the end of the scene (maybe* PETER *joins in).*]

Andante mosso moderatamente

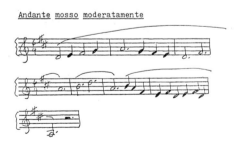

BOB   'Be not afeard. The isle is full of noises, sounds and sweet airs, that give delight and hurt not.'

BET   – 'And then, in dreaming, the clouds methought would open and show riches ready to drop upon me – that, when I wak'd, I cried to dream again!' [*She sits on the beach, not too near the others.*] God, this sand is hard on the skin – on our old skin! You have to be born with skin that's ready for this sand and – salt! For this whole bloody climate! – I'm going then. I'm going ... Pick myself up. and get away. And go.

[*She doesn't move.* LINDA *(and* PETER*) sing, and stare at* BET. BOB *closes his eyes.*]

OTHER PUBLISHED PLAYS BY JOHN MURRELL:

Uncle Vanya (translated from the Russian of Anton Chekhov)
Toronto: Theatrebooks Limited, 1978.
First presented at the Stratford Festival of Canada in 1978, under the direction of Robin Phillips and Urjo Kareda.

Memoir
New York: Avon (Bard) Books, 1978.
Also, London: Granada Publishing Limited, 1980 (in Plays of the Year, volume 48).
First presented at the Guelph (Ontario) Spring Festival in 1977, under the direction of Eric Salmon.

Waiting For The Parade
Vancouver: Talonbooks, 1980.
First presented by Alberta Theatre Projects (Calgary) in 1977, under the direction of Douglas Riske.

Sarah et le cri de la langouste (*Memoir*, translated into French by Georges Wilson)
Paris: L'Avant-Scène, 1983.
First presented at the Théâtre de l'Oeuvre (Paris) in 1982, under the direction of Georges Wilson.

Memoiren (*Memoir*, translated into German by Ute Horstmann)
Berlin: Felix Bloch Erben, 1979.
First presented at the Stadttheater Hildesheim in 1979, under the direction of Pierre Léon.

JOHN MURRELL

John Murrell was born in the United States but completed his formal education and theatre training in Alberta, where he has lived and worked (as teacher, actor and director, as well as playwright) for the past twenty years. His play *Memoir*, about the life and art of Sarah Bernhardt, has been translated into more than fifteen languages and performed in more than twenty-five countries worldwide. *Waiting For The Parade*, concerning the lives of five Calgary women during the Second World War, has been produced in virtually every major Canadian city, as well as on two cross-Canada tours, in New York and in London, England, and was filmed for the CBC (telecast in 1984).

Editor for the Press: Robert Wallace
Typeset in Zapf Book and printed in Canada

For a list of other books
write for our catalogue or
call us at 416) 979-2217

The Coach House Press
401 (rear) Huron Street
Toronto, Canada M5S 2G5